The Case for Character Education

The Case for Character Education

A Developmental Approach

Alan L. Lockwood

Teachers College
Columbia University
New York and London

For Judith

Published by Teachers College Press, 1234 Amsterdam Avenue, New York, NY 10027

Copyright © 2009 by Teachers College, Columbia University

Library of Congress Cataloging-in-Publication Data

Lockwood, Alan L., 1941–
  The case for character education : a developmental approach / Alan L. Lockwood.
    p. cm.
  Includes bibliographical references and index.
  ISBN 978-0-8077-4923-4 (pbk. : alk. paper)
  ISBN 978-0-8077-4924-1 (hardcover : alk. paper)
    1. Moral education—United States. I. Title.
  LC311.L567 2009
  370.11'40973—dc22   2008042655

ISBN 978-0-8077-4923-4 (paper)
ISBN 978-0-8077-4924-1 (cloth)

Printed on acid-free paper

Manufactured in the United States of America

16 15 14 13 12 11 10 09   8 7 6 5 4 3 2 1

Contents

Acknowledgments   vii

Prologue   ix

1. What Is Contemporary Character Education?   1
Establishing a Definition of Contemporary Character Education   1
A Definition of Contemporary Character Education   11

2. The Criticisms of Contemporary Character Education   13
The General Theory   13
The View of Human Nature   14
The View of Values   15
The Psychological Assumptions   22
The Educational Perspective   31
Summary   32

3. Responses to the Criticisms   34
How to Respond   34
Assessing the Soundness of Curricular Criticism   35
Responding to Criticisms of the General Theory   37
Summary   44

4. The Formation of a Developmental Perspective   45
Why We Need a Developmental Perspective   45
An Overview of Developmental Perspectives   47
Erik Erikson's Developmentalism   48
Lawrence Kohlberg's Expansion of Developmentalism   54
Summary   66

5. The Theory of Developmental Character Education   **68**

A Modification of the Definition of Contemporary
    Character Education   68

The Goals of Developmental Character Education   70

Features of Developmental Character Education   71

Highlights of the Theory   77

Why We Need Developmental Character Education   78

6. The Practice of Developmental Character Education   **80**

Developmental Curriculum Content   80

Developmental Instructional Practices   89

Summary   97

Epilogue   **99**

What Is Character Education?   99

The Value of Developmental Character Education   100

A Final Comment   101

References   **103**

Index   **107**

About the Author   **112**

Acknowledgments

I am grateful for the valued comments of my colleagues Professors Diana Hess and James Leming. My wife, Dr. Judith Cassetty, provided both substantive and editorial commentary.

Finally, I was honored and humbled to be an advisee and friend of the late Lawrence Kohlberg. His contributions to our field and to my thinking are inestimable.

Prologue

This book is an argument for developmental character education. In general, character education comprises school-initiated programs designed to improve the quality of values-based behavior and thought for children and adolescents. I contend that current conceptions of character education do not systematically take developmental perspectives into their recommendations for curriculum and instruction. While my argument is contemporary, the reader will see that the scholarly premises, in both social science and philosophy, are well established historically.

Educators often differ on whether and how they believe values education should be adopted and applied. There is no disagreement, however, that schooling is not, should not be, and cannot be value free. We explicitly want our young people to become effective and productive members of society. Good citizenship, of course, requires more than intellectual achievement. On most accounts, good citizenship requires people to treat one another with decency and dignity (Leming, 2001). This objective cannot be met if citizens do not hold values that support it. Theodore Roosevelt is widely quoted on this point. He said: "To educate a person in mind and not in morals is to educate a menace to society" (Lickona, 1991, p. 3). This volume elaborates a view of values education that is critical to pursuing a mission to promote good citizenship.

In the book I explain what contemporary character education is and I identify what I consider to be the strengths of its theory and practice. I also set out some of the more telling criticisms of contemporary character education. Finally, I argue that there are ways that contemporary character education can be significantly improved by appropriately responding to the major criticisms. I also assert it is critical that character educators adopt a developmental perspective. My contention is that the constructive use of a developmental perspective provides guidance for curriculum and instruction that is age appropriate and vital to any widespread success of character education.

At the outset, some terms need to be clarified and defined. Character education is a form of values education. (I will define character education more fully in the next chapter.) Values education is an umbrella phrase that covers a variety of curriculum and instruction practices, different from one another but similar in that they directly deal with values in some fashion. Two of the most notable of these practices are Values Clarification and cognitive-moral development education. These will be elaborated on in subsequent chapters. While there is no officially agreed-upon definition of the term *value*, I define a value as a criterion we employ in making judgments of the worth of a thing, a person, or an action.

There is a distinction between explicit values education and implicit values education. Implicit values education refers to beliefs that schools, partly because of the way they are organized, transmit to students even though they are not part of the official curriculum. Implicit values education frequently is considered part of the "hidden curriculum," a concept attributed to Philip W. Jackson (1990). For example, the differences in status among students and adults reflect, and possibly teach, the roles society expects people to play.

Explicit values education refers to curricula that openly and directly deal with values. Explicit values education means that some treatment of values is part of the official curriculum, not the hidden one. In this volume I will be addressing only explicit values education.

There is no one form of explicit values education. Among the types of explicit values content included in curricula one may find approaches such as inculcation, moral development, analysis, clarification, and action learning (Superka, Ahrens, & Hedstrom, 1976).

Inculcation refers to approaches designed to get students to endorse and act upon specific values and behaviors set by the curriculum. The teacher or the curriculum identifies the values and behaviors it wants pupils to hold and, through the teacher's lecturing, role modeling, reading stories with appropriate morals, and so on, attempts to get students to endorse these values and behaviors.

Moral development entails involving students in the discussion of moral issues so that they may develop more complex, better justified, and sophisticated moral points of view. Students typically read factual or fictional stories in which characters are faced with making judgments of moral right and wrong. The teacher leads students in discussions directed at evaluating the decisions made by the characters and explaining the reasons for students' judgments of the characters' actions.

Values Analysis teaches students the methods of social science and applies them to value questions. Students learn how to create hypotheses, gather and evaluate evidence, and make tentative conclusions on the value questions being examined. For example, students might consider the question of whether the atomic bomb should have been used in World War II. One hypothesis relevant to such considerations is whether the use of the bomb shortened the war. Students would seek evidence to support various answers to the question and consider which answer is best supported by the evidence.

Values Clarification engages students in a process of valuing so that they may choose values that are important to them. Activities are provided that encourage students to think about what is of value to them. The value learnings in this approach are what the students, not the curriculum or the instructor, think is worthwhile. For example, they might identify their favorite TV shows and introspect about how these shows reflect what they value.

Action learning has students determine where they stand on some public value question and teaches them how to influence public policy in their community. For example, students might want traffic lights at some dangerous corners in their town to prevent accidents and injuries. In working to get this policy enacted, they would, among other things, learn who makes these decisions and how they are made. With this knowledge they would prepare and make their case to the appropriate authorities.

A HISTORICAL GLIMPSE AT VALUES EDUCATION

Values education is not a recent curriculum phenomenon. In one form or another it has been part of formal schooling in America since colonial times. Certainly it was part of the educational practices of Native Americans and of early explorers and settlers from Spain and France as well, although I am unaware of historians who have investigated and reported on those practices. In this section I will present a brief history of the role of values in schooling so that the reader will see that values education is not some fleeting contemporary educational fad. A more detailed account of the history of values and American schooling can be found in Smagorinsky and Taxel (2005).

In colonial times explicit values education was closely tied to some form of Protestant religious education. The *New England Primer* mixed religious doctrine into grammar lessons. We are probably all familiar, for example, that in learning the alphabet students recited such epigrams as: A, "In ADAM's Fall, We sinned all."

The Protestant connection to values education in schools persisted well into the 19th century. Horace Mann of Massachusetts, the leading proponent of public education in the United States, firmly believed the Bible should be read in public schools. That century's version of the *New England Primer*, *McGuffey's Reader*, which sold millions of copies, incorporated moral instruction into its lessons.

The Protestant permeation of values education diminished by the end of the century. The relative religious homogeneity of the early nation changed dramatically as vast numbers of immigrants from non-Protestant countries entered the United States to take advantage of jobs in the booming manufacturing industry largely in the northeast. The large numbers of Catholic and Jewish immigrants sought to promote religious values within educational frameworks that were often at odds with the Protestant monopoly on schooling. The resulting values conflict at times became violent, as it did in 1844 in Philadelphia where rioting occurred over Catholic objections to the exclusive use of the Protestant Bible in public schools. The development of Catholic private schools was, in part, a reaction to such issues. Similarly, the settlement house movement and later the YMCA, YWCA, and their Jewish counterparts sought to foster the inculcation of their values as the public schools lost their strong connection to religious values education.

The mode of secular values education most widely promulgated in the early 20th century was called character education. Generally speaking, character education aimed to get young people to hold and act upon certain values, such as honesty, patriotism, and courtesy, often tied to conceptions of good democratic citizenship and a sound work ethic as opposed to religious doctrine and traditions. The character education movement was consistent with the Americanization movement designed to assimilate the growing numbers of immigrants into American culture and democracy. For reasons that are unclear, the widespread, explicit implementation of character education faded from schools as the century moved on. Many of its practices and goals, however, became integrated into the regular school curriculum in both public and parochial schools.

In the 1960s, values education again became a highly visible and strongly advocated movement. The best known and most widely implemented form of values education was Values Clarification (Raths, Harmin, & Simon, 1966). This approach, to be more fully discussed in Chapter 1, had teachers instruct their students in a process of valuing. Teachers were not to teach particular values and strive to inculcate them in students, but rather to facilitate each student's quest for values. The values individual students developed through a carefully delineated clarification process were to help them overcome behaviors and thought processes that were self-destructive and antisocial and to promote their psychological well-being.

Another form of values education emerged in the 1960s as well. Based on the work of developmental psychologist Lawrence Kohlberg, it became known as the moral development approach to values education (Kohlberg, 1970). Kohlberg's research showed that people passed through distinct stages of moral reasoning as they matured. Kohlberg argued that the highest stages of moral reasoning were philosophically superior to the lower stages because the highest stages were based on principles and were concerned with the rights and well-being of others. Lower stage reasoning at Stage 2 was self-centered: What was right was that which served the desires of the individual. Lower stage reasoning at Stage 3 was philosophically inadequate because it was based simply on unexamined custom and tradition.

Further, research showed that not all people naturally matured to the highest stages. Kohlberg found that most adults reasoned at what he called conventional reasoning as opposed to the highest stages of principled reasoning. Encouragingly, research showed that students who engaged in systematic discussion of moral dilemmas developed more fully and rapidly through the stages of moral reasoning than students who did not participate in these discussions. The essence of the moral development approach, to be discussed more thoroughly in Chapter 1, was to engage students in discussion of moral issues as they arose in the content of the curriculum or the life of the school. Kohlberg hoped that his form of values education would produce citizens who addressed moral issues from a principled stance.

By the end of the 20th century both Values Clarification and moral development had faded from prominence. In their place, character education re-emerged as the dominant theory of values education for schools. I refer to this as contemporary character education to distinguish it from the character education movement of the early 19th century.

Contemporary character education advocates are appalled at reported high rates of personally and socially destructive behavior among youth. Advocates claim that such behavior is a result of poor character. One's character is shown by the values one holds. Advocates contend that people with bad character hold bad values and produce bad behavior. People with good character hold good values and engage in good behavior. The general purpose of contemporary character education is to see that young people are inculcated with proper values and engage in appropriate behavior (Lickona, 1991).

As we have seen, values education, in some form or another, has always been a part of formal education in America. These forms have varied in terms of their purposes. Religious forms were intended to instruct and reinforce central tenets of a given religion. The first incarnation of character education aimed at getting students to endorse and act upon a specified set of secular values. Values Clarification aimed at improving the psychological well-being of young people. Moral development's goal was to increase the quality and complexity of moral reasoning. And, more recently, contemporary character education focuses on reducing or eliminating destructive behavior among the young.

THE NEED FOR SOUND VALUES EDUCATION

This historical review showing the various forms that values education has taken over the centuries should not distract us from the critical contemporary need for values education. Education is by its nature a value-laden enterprise with significant moral underpinnings. This is well established in the classic work of R. S. Peters (1967). As he put it, education "implies that something worthwhile is being or has been intentionally transmitted in a morally acceptable manner. It would be a logical contradiction to say that a man had been educated but that he had in no way changed for the better" (p. 3).

Educators are engaged in values education whether they wish to acknowledge it or accept it, or not. What is at stake for our young people and our society is that the best justified and researched values education practices should be made available in our schools.

Schools do more than educate in academic and technical subjects and skills. They also have a pivotal role in helping young people engage in behavior that is of value to themselves and their society. Increasingly, educators and the general public are endorsing the need for effective values education. Elam, Rose, and Gallup (1993) summarize the results of Gallup polls of public attitudes toward schooling: "In 1975, 79% of the public favored instruction in the public schools that would deal with morals and moral behavior. In the 1976 poll, 67% of the respondents said that the public schools should 'take on a share of parents' responsibilities for the moral behavior of their children'" (p. 145). In a 2004 poll by the Center for Civic Education, 75% of respondents said schools should have the goal of "developing positive character traits" (p. 5). Clearly there is public support for this purpose of schooling.

The contemporary character education movement, led most notably by Lickona, Wynne, and Ryan, has significant strengths. For one, it has highlighted the importance of schooling that attempts to have a positive influence on the values and behavior of young people. This message has been presented regularly and has found a receptive audience among school personnel, major national educational organizations, and makers of public policy.

Another notable strength of contemporary character education is that its advocates are immersed in the lives of schoolchildren and their teachers. They are not theorists isolated from the realities of schooling. The advocates spend time in schools, and their writings abound with classroom examples of what they believe to be sound values education practices.

While the message of contemporary character education is clear and direct and its connection to life in schools is admirable, there are questions and criticisms of its approach to values education. My goal is to set forth a conception of character education that takes into account sound criticisms and adds to the theory and practice of character education in ways I believe will have a significant and positive impact on this form of values education.

This book sets forth an argument for developing a soundly justified approach to values education. As the reader will see, this is not a simple matter.

Careful examination of arguments, rationales, and research is required. It is a complex effort but one that is worthwhile and vitally important.

WHAT IS TO COME

In the remainder of this volume I look carefully at contemporary character education. I assess the strengths and weaknesses of this approach to values education. I then recommend substantial modifications of and additions to the theory and practice of contemporary character education. I must reiterate that this book is an argument for developmental character education and not a comprehensive review of recent literature. Such literature is used, where appropriate, to clarify the argument.

In Chapter 1, I establish a definition of contemporary character education. There are an extraordinary number of programs and materials that claim the mantle of character education. The values education landscape is strewn with these highly varied and often mutually contradictory curricula. By examining the works of the leading advocates for contemporary character education, I develop a definition of character education that captures what it is and what it is not. This definition helps school leaders who wish to establish programs in character education or purchase curriculum materials. The definition helps program evaluators seeking to assess the effectiveness of character education. The definition is also of value to critical analysts examining the soundness of character education theory and practice.

In Chapter 2, I engage in a critical analysis of contemporary character education. Among the criticisms leveled against contemporary character education are:

1. The emphasis on rewards and punishments is an application of an incorrect psychology of learning
2. The claim that bad behavior is a consequence of holding bad values fails to take into account social and economic forces that influence behavior
3. The presumption that behavior flows directly from values is not supported by research
4. Character education advocates fail to consider the differences between adolescents and young children when setting forth recommended practices
5. There is a tendency to see value-based decisions as simply right or wrong and little recognition of complex situations in which good values can come into apparent conflict with one another

6. Character education is seen as ennobling the political, social, and economic status quo

In Chapter 3, I discuss how character education should respond to these criticisms. I contend that contemporary character education advocates should take these criticisms seriously and examine them in a logical manner following established conceptions of scholarly inquiry. It is the responsible thing to do. This does not mean, however, that all criticisms are equally telling. Some criticisms, for example, may be so highly theoretical or ideological that they would not have a clear or significant effect on practice. In this chapter I weigh the criticisms on logical and scientific grounds and identify those that have been or should be examined further.

One of the frequent criticisms of character education is that its advocates do not take seriously the developmental differences between young children and older adolescents. In Chapter 4, I consider two well-regarded developmental perspectives, both of which were developed by psychologists. The purpose is to demonstrate how these developmental perspectives can inform modifications and enhancements to contemporary character education. Primarily, I review the developmental psychologies of Erik Erikson and Lawrence Kohlberg. These two psychologies have much to say about the developmental differences of students as they move through their school years. In my analysis I assess how features of these developmental perspectives productively can shape the theory and practice of character education.

In Chapter 5, I highlight the central features of the case for developmental character education. My argument includes a refinement of the definition of character education and an elaboration of the goals of developmental character education. Chapter 5 also addresses central tenets of the proposed approach and how it addresses substantive criticisms of contemporary character education.

Chapter 6 includes illustrations of the practice of developmental character education. Although there is no "official" curriculum and instruction for developmental character education, there are practices that are consistent with its goals and rationale. In no way should this chapter or book be understood to be a fully explicated character education curriculum. I intend it as a frame of reference for school leaders and curriculum developers making decisions about what approach to character education they wish to endorse, adopt, or design.

The Epilogue provides some closing commentary about the case for developmental character education. It ends by restating the hope that a developmental perspective can provide a profound service to character education for our young people and society.

Chapter 1

What Is Contemporary Character Education?

The concept of contemporary character education is difficult to define. Even a cursory glance at commercially available character education curriculum materials reveals a remarkable array of strikingly different approaches. For example, I recall attending a character education convention some years ago and, as I moved from room to room, I was struck by the extraordinary variety of topics and practices being presented and all claiming to be character education. It was as though some viral distortion of postmodernism had infected the field; character education was whatever anyone said it was.

Is character education a label without a referent? Let us hope not. There are government and foundation grants available to support character education in both program design and application; there are organizations devoted to promoting character education; there are conventions addressing character education; there are books and articles about character education; there is a *Journal of Research in Character Education*. Surely character education must be something identifiable; otherwise, how could it be funded, practiced, researched, and discussed?

The reader may accuse me of assembling a straw man. After all, if there are articles, conventions, organizations, grants, and programs dealing with character education, it must have an agreed-upon meaning. One might think so. Unfortunately, that is not the case. To illustrate this I encourage the reader to search the Internet under the heading "character education." In moments you will see the astonishing array of materials and organizations related to character education. The definition of contemporary character education is elusive but, as I will show, its substantive features can be delineated.

ESTABLISHING A DEFINITION OF CONTEMPORARY CHARACTER EDUCATION

A useful way to establish a definition of contemporary character education is to examine the writings of its major advocates. (I use *contemporary* to distinguish the current movement from that of the early 20th century.) While these advocates do not set out an agreed-upon, established definition of character education, I believe one can be deduced from the arguments they make and the policies they endorse.

Although a number of advocates have written about character education, three men have been recognized as the central leaders of the contemporary movement: Thomas Lickona of SUNY–Cortland, Kevin Ryan of Boston University, and the late Edward Wynne of the University of Illinois–Chicago. It is primarily their writings that I will sift through in developing a working definition of character education. First I will set out what they see as the major purpose(s) and arguments for character education, in short, its rationale. Second, I will describe the educational applications that they endorse. I then will compare their prescriptions for the practice of contemporary character education with two other approaches to values education. Finally, after this explication and analysis, I will offer a definition of character education that is broad enough to encompass a variety of current practices but narrow enough to allow us to say what it is and what it is not.

The Aim of Contemporary Character Education

Put most simply, character education advocates want their programs to promote positive ethical behavior among young people and reduce or eliminate socially and personally destructive behavior. There are ancillary aims as well, but the central goal is to establish good behavior among our youth.

At the outset of *Educating for Character*, Lickona (1991) points to signs of a moral decline in our society and focuses on distressing statistics showing negative behavior among young people. He describes alarming statistics on murder rates and vandalism among young people; he offers evidence of widespread stealing and cheating; he identifies trends of racism, bullying, and disrespect for authorities; he highlights self-destructive behaviors such as drug and alcohol use and trends in teen suicide.

Lickona (2004) sums up the need for character education: "The premise of the character education movement is that the disturbing behaviors that bombard us daily—violence, greed, corruption, incivility, drug abuse, sexual immorality, and a poor work ethic—have a common core: the absence of good character" (p. xxiii). Lickona and his fellow character education advocates are not alone. Hart and Carlo (2005) report that almost 75% of adults, when asked to describe adolescents, use adjectives suggesting moral deficiencies.

Professor Wynne has characterized these negative behavioral trends as evidence of substantial disorder among American youth. With his colleague Jacques Benninga he echoes Lickona's concern about the behavior of young people. For them, character education is needed to combat youth homicide, out-of-wedlock births, and a variety of other destructive behavior. They endorse character education for youth because "we want them to stop killing and abusing themselves and one another at record rates" (Benninga & Wynne, 1998, pp. 439–440).

Wynne and Kevin Ryan (1997) set out a similar rationale. "As we will see, a variety of measures show there has been a substantial, long-term decline in the conduct of young Americans" (p. 7). They go on to cite statistics similar to those of Lickona on poor behavior among youth as evidence of the need for character education.

William J. Bennett (1993), former U.S. Secretary of Education, has been a long-time supporter of character education. In part to bolster the argument for character education, he assisted in the publication of a booklet of statistics that, he claims, document increasing social and moral decline. He offers statistics on juvenile violent crime, teen pregnancy, teen suicide, and drug use.

As the above litany of presumed social woes among young people indicates, proponents of character education intend their programs and policies to reduce or eliminate these destructive behaviors. This is the most oft-stated aim of character education by its key advocates.

The Presumed Need for Good Character

The proponents of character education are not, of course, the only persons concerned with personally and socially destructive behavior. All thoughtful adults are distressed by such behavior. What is distinctive among character education advocates is their argument for addressing these behaviors.

For the advocates, these social ills are a consequence of young people's poor character. The proponents of character education say little about the social, political, and economic contexts in which these behaviors emerge. Some critics of character education focus on this: "The basic explanation that the character education movement offers for moral decline is a psychological one, that the problems are rooted in an inflated sense of personalism and self-centeredness rather than in social, economic, and cultural institutions" (Purpel, 1997, p. 150).

Proponents of character education are not ignorant of the context in which these behaviors occur, but they say little about it. For them, poor behavior is the result of poor character: "The roots of such conduct are properly perceived as character related" (Wynne, 1989, p. 24). For contemporary character educators, the source of identified social ills lies with persons, and the reform of persons through character education is the way to address the problems. "We are coming to see that our societal moral problems reflect, in no small measure, our personal vices" (Lickona, 1991, p. 49). For the advocates, positive behavior will come about when good character is instilled or nurtured in the young.

For character education advocates, good character is intimately intertwined with good values. For them, people are not born with these values; they have to be learned. In a healthy society, the major social institutions, such as the family and schools, transmit these values to the young. When a society shows moral decay, as ours allegedly does, it is largely a consequence of the failure of social institutions to effectively transmit good moral values. Wynne (1985/1986) refers to this transmission as "the great tradition" and claims that all societies properly engage in it in order to maintain their cultures (pp. 4–9).

For Wynne, the tradition focused on teaching the young appropriate behaviors such as telling the truth and honoring parents. The instructional emphasis was on behavior, not simply the exhortatory teaching of ideas about morality. Also, these character-teaching traditions recommended sustained reinforcement of socially defined proper moral behavior. This instruction was a responsibility of all social institutions. In addition to reinforcement, according to Wynne, the tradition sought to suppress wrong conduct through punishment and other negative sanctions.

The values to be transmitted and acted upon are based on what character education advocates regard as a broad moral consensus. This presumed consensus is an essential justification for the inculcation of such values. That is, there is broad social agreement on what constitutes good values. Therefore, it is warranted that these values be imparted to the young. These values are claimed to be important in promoting healthy personal development, caring relationships, social order, and justice.

Lickona (1991) identifies two foundational moral values, respect and responsibility. Respect shows concern for the worth of the self and others. Responsibility involves active engagement in worthwhile behaviors and developing personal characteristics, such as dependability, and carrying out our duties and commitments. There are many other values, largely derived from these two, that should be included in any list of desirable values. Among them are honesty, fairness, tolerance, helpfulness, compassion, courage, and self-discipline. There are also values inherent in democracy. These include equality of opportunity, due process, the rule of law, and the like. Because they are central to our democracy, they too should be taught directly.

For Lickona (1991), good character involves more than holding or endorsing particular moral values. There are three major components of good character: moral knowing, moral feeling, and moral action. In essence, a person with good character knows what is good, appreciates what is good, and acts upon what is good.

The Means of Character Education

So far we have seen that character education proponents intend their programs to diminish destructive behavior among young people. They believe that such behavior is best treated by promoting good character in the young. Stated generally, people of good character hold worthwhile values and act on the basis of those values.

Now we turn to the means of character education. What are the practices set forth as most likely to be effective in instilling these values in youth and ensuring they will be manifest in appropriate behavior?

While the proponents of character education generally agree on its aims and the meaning of good character, there is somewhat less consensus on means and methods for promoting good character. Wynne and Ryan favor didactic instruction and the use of rewards and punishments as their preferred practice. Lickona appears to be more flexible.

Wynne and Ryan (1997) recommend an extensive list of practices for schools to implement. They emphasize that schools should clearly establish, publish, and enforce strict rules of acceptable and unacceptable behavior in and out of the classroom. Adults are to accept the role of moral authority and regularly tell students what good behavior is and reward them when they exhibit it and sanction them when they do not.

Wynne and Ryan would have students engage in many simple direct behaviors such as befriending a new student, picking up litter in hallways, helping other students with schoolwork or other activities, and actively participating in school ceremonies such as saying the Pledge of Allegiance. They emphasize that schools should have assemblies and ceremonies in which students who have exhibited identifiable good behavior are praised and rewarded.

In developing an understanding of Wynne and Ryan's stance on the preferred means for character education, it is helpful to see what they reject. For example, they oppose movements to help students develop good self-esteem. Such efforts are most likely to promote self-centeredness in students, they say. For Wynne and Ryan, healthy self-esteem should derive from students' knowledge that they have been diligent and good and have worked hard. Self-esteem is a consequence of such behaviors, not an end in itself. They also question many pedagogical practices associated with the cooperative-learning movement, as well as efforts to create school democracies. For them, cooperative-learning practices diminish appropriate adult authority and give students too much power.

While Lickona (1993) shares many of Wynne and Ryan's recommendations, his list of approved practices is more wide-ranging. For example, he has called upon teachers to model caregiving and good behavior, urged them to teach students to demonstrate respect for one another, recommended creating a democratic classroom in which students help make the classroom a better environment for learning, encouraged the use of cooperative learning, and endorsed practices that promote moral reflection.

I have suggested elsewhere (Lockwood, 1993) that some of Lickona's (1991) prescriptions appear to be internally contradictory. For example, on the one hand, he is a powerful and outspoken supporter of sexual abstinence among unmarried youth. On the other hand, he has advocated values-related educational strategies that encourage open discussion and decision making by students. His adherence to absolute prohibition in some cases would appear at odds with support of practices that encourage individual decision making.

There is no set of pedagogical practices or curriculum materials that is officially endorsed by character education advocates. Character education embraces a variety of instructional practices. As we work to construct a definition of character education, we cannot say it is identified with any particular program of curriculum and instruction. However, this is not to say that any practice can count as character education, as appeared to be the case at the character education conference I mentioned earlier. In fact, there may be many practices consistent with contemporary character education, but they are not an unbounded, open-ended, limitless array.

So far, in our quest for definition, I have presented an outline of the aims of character education and its advocates' conception of what constitutes good character. These are matters endorsed by the proponents. We also can sharpen our understanding of contemporary character education by examining what modes of values education its advocates reject.

Character Education Versus Values Clarification

Values Clarification is an approach to values education that was first established in 1966 by Raths, Harmin, and Simon. (Please note the capital letters. This is to distinguish the Raths approach from values clarification in general.) Many curricula involve the clarification of students' values, but Raths's Values Clarification is a specific approach. Numerous volumes and articles about Values Clarification followed over the years. Many subsequent books contained scores of specific daily lesson plans that were easy for teachers to incorporate into their curricular schedules. Values Clarification was adopted widely both here and abroad. In spite of its popularity, as we will see, it was roundly rejected by many scholars as well as advocates of character education.

Up to a point, the rationale for Values Clarification resembles that of character education. The creators of Values Clarification offered their list of problems, such as apathy and overdissention among youth, and contended that young people did not hold useful, functional values:

> Could it be, we wonder, that the pace and complexity of modern life has so exacerbated the problem of deciding what is good and what is right and what is worthy and what is desirable that large numbers of children are finding it increasingly bewildering, even overwhelming, to decide what is worth valuing, what is worth one's time and energy? (Raths, Harmin, & Simon, 1966, p. 7)

Unlike contemporary character educators, however, Values Clarification proponents explicitly contend that social conditions contribute to the difficulty young people have in establishing values. They speak to the diminished role of religion in the lives of many; they speak of distrust of political leaders; they speak of divorce rates and broken families; they speak of the many varying, often negative value messages that youth are peppered with by the media.

The proponents of Values Clarification believe there are negative consequences of values confusion. Among the consequences are young people who are *"apathetic, flighty, uncertain,* or *inconsistent,* or who are *drifters, overconformers, overdissenters,* or *role players* (Raths, Harmin, & Simon, 1966, p. 7, emphasis in original). Although contemporary character education came much later than Values Clarification, it would appear that their rationales are more similar than not regarding the effects of the possession of inadequate values.

In short, the advocates of both character education and Values Clarification claim that young people have various behavior problems and that these problems are attributable to lack of values. The task for values educators is to see that young people develop appropriate values. At this point contemporary character education parts ways with Values Clarification.

Character education defines the specific values that young people should hold, whereas Values Clarification does not. Rather, Values Clarification aims to teach students a process through which they can formulate their own values. When students arrive at their own conclusions and define their own values, negative behavior presumably diminishes and persons become "positive, purposeful, enthusiastic, and proud" (Raths, Harmin, & Simon, 1966, p. 12).

The process that leads to the articulation of a value under Values Clarification derives from the proponents' definition of what constitutes a value. They indicate that their strict definition makes it clear that people do not hold many values. Students' initial attitudes, interests, feelings, and the like, are called value indicators. They become values only if they meet all seven of the criteria for what constitutes a "true" value according to the definition. In the Values Clarification model, a true value must be:

1. Chosen freely
2. Chosen from alternatives
3. Chosen after thoughtful consideration of the consequences of each alternative
4. Prized and cherished
5. Publicly affirmed
6. Acted upon
7. Acted upon repeatedly (Raths, Harmin, & Simon, 1966, p. 30)

The process of achieving a value, in essence, involves assessing whether one's beliefs and behaviors meet all seven of these criteria. In the classroom, the teacher employs a variety of teaching methods called strategies. These strategies require students to think carefully about their ideas and behaviors to see whether they reach the level of a value as opposed to a mere value indicator.

Strategies may address one or more of the seven criteria. For example, a strategy called consequences search has students set out a number of possible alternatives for dealing with a problem. Students then brainstorm the likely consequences of each alternative. Finally they consider which alternative is best in light of its consequences (Simon, Howe, & Kirschenbaum, 1972).

Clearly, Values Clarification is designed to equip students to think deeply about themselves and their experiences in order to determine what they value. The teacher's task is to facilitate introspection and discussion, not to assert or inculcate specific values that students should hold. The teacher is to lead a classroom in which he or she is nonjudgmental, nurturing, tolerant of many points of view, and respectful of all students' contributions to discussions. Also, the teacher is to create a classroom climate in which students are respectful of one another and do not in engage in arguments with one another regarding the superiority of one value choice over another. Ideally, students learn to employ clarifying responses with one another.

Earlier, I mentioned that contemporary character education advocates, and others, have substantive reservations about the efficacy of the Values Clarification approach to values education. The primary reason for these reservations centers on the exponents' emphasis on value neutrality, which appears to present the possibility that it promotes ethical relativism as its implicit moral point of view.

In its values-related classroom strategies, Values Clarification makes no distinction between moral values and nonmoral values. (Please note that the term *nonmoral values* does not mean "immoral values." This is an important distinction.) We all have preferences (values) for a variety of things, actions, and policies. When our preferences involve the fundamental rights and well-being of others, we call them moral values. When our preferences involve such things as entertainment, foods, fashions, and the like, we call them nonmoral values. We hope that moral value decisions, because they affect fundamental human rights, will be made carefully, thoughtfully, and with sound justifications. On the other hand, we tolerate a wide range of nonmoral value choices and, compared with moral decisions, we have less concern with how they are made. We do not have a deep human stake in how nonmoral decisions are made. If one prefers French cuisine to Thai, that's one's opinion and so be it. We certainly would not characterize such a choice as immoral or moral, as we would one's views on, say, capital punishment, where human life is at stake.

One of the Values Clarification strategies, values voting, illustrates how Values Clarification fails to make the nonmoral versus moral value distinction. In this strategy students are asked their views on such moral value issues as cheating and capital punishment and on nonmoral values such as preferred deodorant and favorite hobbies (Simon, Howe, & Kirschenbaum, 1972). This mixing of types of values gives the impression that making decisions about capital punishment and selection of deodorant should be made in the same manner.

The failure to distinguish moral from nonmoral value types is a serious problem for Values Clarification, as it takes the position that the same process for making value decisions should be applied to both moral and nonmoral questions. The choosing, prizing, and acting process is to be applied to decisions affecting human life and decisions regarding what type of movie one wishes to see. There is no sense that the former demands weighty consideration, while the latter, from a moral point of view, is relatively trivial.

The seven-step process promulgated by the advocates of Values Clarification is intended to help individuals determine what they personally value. It does not require any justification for their choices beyond the seven criteria. This has led critics to say that Values Clarification promotes ethical relativism (Lockwood, 1975). Put most simply, ethical relativism is the doctrine that one moral value decision cannot be shown to be better than any other. Character education advocates, and other critics of Values Clarification, reject ethical relativism because it leads people to believe that any moral choice they make, whether prosocial or antisocial, is justified because it cannot be definitively proven wrong. For them, rejecting ethical relativism is tantamount to rejecting Values Clarification.

Of relativism, Lickona (1991) states firmly:

> Such thinking fails to grasp a fundamental moral truth. There *are* rationally grounded, nonrelative, objectively worthwhile moral values: respect for human life, liberty, the inherent value of every individual person, and the consequent

responsibility to care for each other and carry out our basic obligations. (p. 230, emphasis in original)

Character Education Versus Moral Development

In pursuit of a working definition of contemporary character education, I have set out various curricular features the advocates endorse. I then compared character education with Values Clarification to illustrate the features of one well-known values education program that character education proponents reject. Now I will compare character education with the moral development approach to values education.

The moral development approach to values education derives from the work of Lawrence Kohlberg and his colleagues. Kohlberg was a developmental psychologist whose work was stimulated by Jean Piaget's (1965) research on the moral thinking of young people. Piaget posited the view that profound changes occur in people's moral thinking as they mature. Their thinking moves through stages. He identified two major stages of moral development: moral heteronomy and moral autonomy. Kohlberg chose to examine the development of moral thinking in much greater depth than did Piaget.

Kohlberg's original research was a longitudinal study. He interviewed subjects on a series of moral dilemmas created as vignettes in which a character makes a major moral decision. For example, in the famous Heinz dilemma, Heinz's wife is dying of cancer. The druggist in town has a drug that might save her life but is charging much more money than Heinz can afford. The druggist refuses to lower his price for Heinz, and Heinz cannot raise the money in any way. One night Heinz breaks into the store and steals the drug. In Kohlberg's interview design, each subject is asked whether what Heinz did was right or wrong and to explain his or her reasons for the decision.

Kohlberg found that subjects' reasoning changed substantively over time. For example, younger subjects might focus on the harm that might come to Heinz if he was caught. For them, what is important is whether he can get away with the crime. In young adulthood, subjects might focus on the druggist's property rights in relationship to Heinz's wife's right to life and the laws against stealing. What is important for these older subjects is balancing competing moral rights in the situation.

Kohlberg called these changes in moral reasoning stages of moral development. Each stage was, in effect, characterized by an identifiable moral philosophy that subjects brought to bear on moral dilemmas used in the interviews. Kohlberg (1970) initially claimed there were six stages of moral reasoning. Later in this volume I will explicate Kohlberg's psychology of moral development in more detail. Here, however, we are interested mainly in the values education program that grew out of his work so that we can examine how it is viewed by character education advocates.

According to Kohlberg, not all people develop to the highest stages. Most adults reason predominantly at Stages 3 and 4. Kohlberg and his colleagues were distressed by this finding because, as Kohlberg had argued, the highest stages represented forms of moral reasoning that were philosophically superior to the earlier stages (Kohlberg, 1971). From a moral point of view, he argued it would be best if people reasoned at the highest stages. Many wondered whether some educational intervention could stimulate development or whether one's final level of development was not subject to external influences.

One of Kohlberg's students, Moshe Blatt, thought that instruction during which students systematically discussed moral dilemmas might advance their development faster than would occur without such discussion. In his study, the experimental group had a statistically significant advance in moral reasoning compared with control groups (Blatt & Kohlberg, 1971). The growth in scores measuring moral reasoning was relatively small but was sustained over time after the experiments ended. Such results led curriculum developers familiar with Kohlberg's work to advocate and design instructional programs emphasizing student discussion of moral dilemmas and issues, with an expectation that such an approach to values education would stimulate student moral reasoning development to the preferred higher stages of moral reasoning.

As with Values Clarification, most leading character education advocates reject the moral development approach to values education. The opposition to Kohlberg's instructional practices was based largely on the fact that moral development instructors did not inculcate specific values or behaviors. Instead they engaged students in a process of deep discussion of moral issues. Character education proponents typically want teachers to have a leading role in directly teaching key moral values (Wynne & Ryan, 1997).

A DEFINITION OF
CONTEMPORARY CHARACTER EDUCATION

Given this explication of the beliefs of prominent contemporary character education advocates and a look at practices they reject, we can come closer to a definition of contemporary character education. We have seen that character education advocates share the following beliefs:

1. The central goal of contemporary character education is to promote positive behavior among youth and to diminish or eliminate personal and socially destructive behavior.
2. Good behavior is the consequence of having proper values. Bad behavior is the consequence of holding incorrect values or, perhaps, holding no values at all.
3. People who hold proper values and act on those values have good character.
4. The moral point of view called ethical relativism is rejected. There are moral rights and wrongs.
5. There are a variety of instructional practices that can promote good character. Generally speaking, these practices involve direct instruction in what values to hold and examples of how to act upon them.

By my analysis, for a program accurately to be called character education it must possess all five of these characteristics as enunciated by the leading proponents of contemporary character education. If the program does not possess all of these features, it is something else. It may be a fine program, but it is not character education. Thus, my definition of character education:

> Character education is any school-directed program designed to shape directly and systematically the behavior of young people by teaching explicitly the nonrelativistic values believed to directly bring about good behavior. (Lockwood, 1997, p. 179)

This derivation of a definition helps us understand the central features of contemporary character education theory and practice. This definition is assumed in the remainder of this volume when I refer to character education.

In the next chapter I will examine criticisms of contemporary character education. To the extent there are sound criticisms, they can help us obtain a richer understanding of contemporary character education and, more important, aid us in shaping a more adequate rationale for its theory and practice.

Chapter 2

The Criticisms of Contemporary Character Education

Chapter 1 establishes a working definition of contemporary character education. In this chapter, I will describe the major criticisms of character education. Because the goal of this book is to refine and explicate a conception of character education intended to increase the probability that worthwhile goals will be realized, it is important to gain an understanding of the perceived weaknesses of character education's theory and practice. In this chapter I divide the criticisms into two general categories: criticisms of the general theory and criticisms of the psychological assumptions that undergird the theory and recommended practices. In Chapter 3, I will assess the soundness of these criticisms. I believe that curriculum advocates have a responsibility to respond to sound criticisms of their positions. Consequently, I suggest how character education should respond to sound criticisms.

THE GENERAL THEORY

To summarize the description of contemporary character education set out in the previous chapter, character education advocates bemoan the high rates of destructive behavior among young people. They cite statistics indicating that such undesirable behavior is either at very high rates or rising. The pivotal claim of the advocates is that this behavior is a direct consequence of the poor character of youth. To diminish or eliminate this destructive behavior schools must promote good character among young people.

For character education advocates, good character means holding good values, recognizing these values as worthwhile, and acting upon them (Lickona, 1991). For character education advocates, the values that should be held reflect a social and historical consensus about what is good for people and society. Their list includes such values as respect, honesty, responsibility, courtesy, loyalty, and obedience to authority.

The values that constitute good character are to be directly taught to young people. Contemporary character education advocates believe that responsible adults know what values are good. Character education does not engage students in discussions of what they think good values are. The issue is how to get those values embedded into students' consciousness and behavior patterns. "The point is that, on the whole, school is and should and must be inherently indoctrinative. The only significant questions are: Will the indoctrination be overt or covert, and what will be indoctrinated" (Wynne, 1985/1986, p. 9).

THE VIEW OF HUMAN NATURE

Some critics, Kohn (1997), for example, have taken issue with what they see as contemporary character education advocates' bleak assessment of human nature. They see it as a version of the Christian doctrine of original sin. Wynne (1985/1986) is perhaps the clearest on this when he speaks of a presumed "great tradition" of transmitting social values: "The tradition had a pessimistic opinion about the perfectibility of human beings" (p. 7). Philosophically, this stance is most consistent with that of Thomas Hobbes, the 17th-century English philosopher who proposed the need for a powerful government to control the natural brutish, antisocial, selfishness of humans. This view, as applied to children, is dramatically captured in William Golding's 1954 classic, *Lord of the Flies*.

To one degree or another, most contemporary character education advocates appear to hold this view either explicitly or implicitly (Kohn, 1997). By no means does this mean that character educators fear children or dislike them. The point is, they would say, that young people must be instructed directly in what to value and how to control themselves for their own good and the good of others. This is claimed to be in the best interest of youth as well as society.

Contemporary character educators believe children cannot learn how to control their impulses by themselves. Their learning environment must be organized in particular ways and direct instruction must instill the values that yield appropriate behavior:

> A learner's internal state is largely shaped by directing his [sic] behavior. The theories underlying such shaping may be termed 'sophisticated behaviorism' and/or social learning: the systemic—but still semi-tacit mobilization of the forces in the environment to form appropriate behaviors. (Wynne, 1997, p. 65)

From the critics' perspective, this concern with social disorder, presumably instigated by character-deficient youth, leads contemporary character education advocates to endorse a politically conservative agenda crying out for social stability. By tying social disorder to character failings, character education advocates fail to consider seriously the influence of the social, economic, and political contexts in which such behavior occurs.

These attributes of contemporary character education discourse lead critics to berate advocates for failing to take seriously matters of social, political, and economic justice:

> Implicit in such a discourse is the assumption that our social problems are not so much rooted in the failures of our social, economic, and political structures as in the attitudes and behaviors of individuals. (Purpel, 1997, p. 140)

At their worst, character education advocates seem blind to widespread, often institutionalized inequalities and injustices that may contribute to social disorder. Vast and growing disparities in income and wealth are not taken seriously. The grinding, stultifying effects of poverty do not appear in their picture of society. The persistent influences of racism and sexism are apparently not with us.

This is not to say that individuals have no responsibility for their behavior. The argument is that contemporary character education downplays the effects of social, economic, and political conditions on behavior and says little about specific contextual influences on behavior (Purpel, 1997). For contemporary character education advocates, the linchpin to a stable, hopefully just society is the good character of youth. The key to realizing this good behavior is the installation of proper values in the young.

Interestingly, on this count, no critic of contemporary character education has brought forth the notion that some destructive behavior is a consequence of psychological disorder, not the result of holding poor values or living in a difficult environment. Because this argument has not been made in the debates over character education, I will not develop it here. It is worth noting, however, that this position is held by prominent researchers examining effective programs for addressing problem behavior: "The promotion of children's social, emotional, behavioral, and cognitive development began to be seen as key to preventing problem behaviors themselves" (Catalano et al., 2004, p. 100).

THE VIEW OF VALUES

One criticism (Lockwood, 1985/1986) of the general theory of contemporary character education advocates is their apparent belief that a social/historical consensus on what values are worthwhile is relatively easy to come by. Wynne (1985/1986) was particularly adamant about this supposed grand historical consensus, which he called "the great tradition."

There certainly is a rich tradition in moral philosophy. Whether it is a great one is a matter of opinion. It clearly is not, however, a tradition resting upon consensus. Western moral philosophy is saturated with profound disagreements. Did Plato and Aristotle share the same views? Did Kant and Mill share the same views? Do teleologists (those who focus on the outcomes of an action to determine its moral value), deontologists (those who focus on the nature of an act to determine its moral value), and relativists (those who do not believe there is moral truth) share the same views? The answer is unequivocally no:

> Only a highly selective reading of the history of Western philosophy could lead one to conclude there is historical agreement on the nature of morality or on a consensually prescribed code of conduct. (Lockwood, 1985/1986, pp. 9-10)

Another line of criticism raised about contemporary character education concerns its philosophical conceptions about how value issues arise in life circumstances. I should point out here that this realm of criticism is not about notions of how values function in human behavior. Those psychological assumptions will be addressed in the next section.

A fundamental criticism of contemporary character education advocates' philosophical view of values is that it is overly simplistic. As we have seen numerous times, they see the central educative task as getting young people to hold proper values. Presumably this will lead to responsible behavior. In fact, determining how values should inform behavior is far more philosophically and psychologically complex than that.

Character education advocates do not discuss issues associated with the meaning of a particular value in general or in specific situations. They are inclined to produce lists of honorific values that, superficially, appear admirable and uncontroversial. Although there is some variation among value lists, one commonly sees such values as honesty, integrity, respect, loyalty, obedience, courtesy, diligence, responsibility, courage, and compassion.

Most people probably agree that the values on any particular list sound worthy and good. Who could be opposed to honesty and courtesy? Disagreements will arise, however, when we try to determine more precisely what the values mean. Generally speaking, character education advocates do not engage students in serious deliberations about the meaning of specific values nor do they elaborate their own views on the meaning of the values. This is a critical hole in the theory because without a clear meaning for a value, it is difficult to know whether we are confronting situations in which the value is at stake and in which some kind of values-based behavior is required.

For example, consider the value of honesty. What does it mean? On one generally agreed-upon reading, honesty means being truthful. However, this does not tell us what to be truthful about, or in what circumstances it would be good or right to tell the truth, or in what circumstances we are obligated to tell the truth. Are we to be truthful about our feelings? Our ideas and opinions? Our personal history? Our future plans? Similarly, are we to be truthful spontaneously in virtually all situations or only in specific situations or only when we are directly called upon to tell the truth? Reasonable answers to these questions may be forthcoming from inquiry and analysis. The point is, however, most character education advocates do not argue for such discussions with students nor do they develop their own arguments.

The simple assertion of and agreement with a value also masks the question of what might be called the degrees or dimensions of a value. Unlike numbers, values are not concrete, stable things. In simple arithmetic, the number 2 is the number 2. If it has variations, they can be stated numerically as 2¼ or 2½, and so on. The degrees of values, of course, cannot be stated so precisely. It makes no sense to say honesty and a half. We can, however, sensibly ask how honest we must be in order to be exhibiting the value of honesty. One can imagine how honesty could reach a point where an extreme degree of truthfulness would yield what some reasonably might believe to be discourtesy or tiresome narcissism.

One can imagine excesses, and undoubtedly deficits, in the expressions of values. Take loyalty, for example. Leaving aside the question of loyalty to what, we readily employ such concepts as blind loyalty and slavish obedience as forms of loyalty that are of questionable value, if not dysfunctional. Or, on the other hand, wavering loyalty or fair weather allegiance are other forms of loyalty that we disparage. As another example, consider diligence or hard work, both widely touted by most character education advocates. At what point does one's admirable diligence become dysfunctional "workaholicism"? This issue of degree can be raised about all values.

To reiterate, the simple assertion of a value does not resolve important questions of what the value means. The question of meaning is not just something for philosophers to examine; it is a critical part of what we must do in deciding how a value should be applied in life. Consequently, it is a vital part of establishing good character. Critics contend that contemporary character educators generally avoid this discussion with students and that, if they understood fully the nature of values, they would not.

The meaning of particular values is not a settled matter. These meanings must be worked out in discussion and analysis as well as in the specific contexts in which they arise. What also is not settled in contemporary character education advocates' view of values is the problematic nature of determining how to act in situations in which values are at stake.

As we will see, deciding what action is right in a situation in which good values come into conflict, as in the Heinz dilemma, is no simple matter. The same is true of some situations in which only one value is centrally involved. Imagine the following, somewhat extreme hypothetical: A family can barely make ends meet. The father runs a fruit stand. One day he asks his 12-year-old daughter to tend the stand and make sure no one takes any fruit while he takes her ill mother to the doctor. While the daughter is caring for the business, a few police officers approach and ask for free apples. Character educators have taught her to obey legitimate authority. She is uncertain what to do. Should she obey her father or the officers of the law? Simple adherence to the value of obedience does not generate a solution to her dilemma (Lockwood, 1993).

Philosophers and social scientists have long known that endorsement of highly generalized statements of values fails to determine action unequivocally when questions arise about how they apply in concrete situations. Myrdal's (1944) classic work provides a perfect illustration of this. Hypothetical examples, such as the fruit stand, are not the only way to illustrate this point. For example, those who support abortion rights claim to value life. Those who oppose abortion rights also claim to value life. Clearly, endorsement of the value of life does not lead to consensus on the propriety of abortion.

The problem of determining right action based on values is particularly acute when values come into conflict. Fictionally this is easily illustrated in Heinz's dilemma, mentioned earlier, which is derived from the character Valjean in *Les Miserables* and employed by Lawrence Kohlberg (Reimer, Paolitto, & Hersh, 1983). To reiterate, in this story, set in an imaginary European country, Heinz's wife is dying of some form of cancer. A druggist in town has a medicine that probably will save her life. The druggist is charging much more for the drug than Heinz can afford, and he will not reduce his price in spite of Heinz's pleas. Heinz is unable to raise the money from friends and other sources. One night he breaks into the drug store and steals the drug. This dilemma illustrates how generally accepted good values can come into conflict in difficult situations. The Heinz story involves appraisal of such values as property rights, obedience to law, and the value of life. Each value, in itself, generally is regarded as worthwhile, but it is in specific contexts that value conflict and ambiguity result.

Fictional stories can illustrate how value conflicts can arise and not be resolved easily. Real life, of course, is replete with issues in which values conflict. These can be prosaic: For instance, when asked whether I like someone's new hair style, and I don't, should I be honest and say so, or should I be courteous and lie? They also can be matters of public policy: For example, should public safety be supported by holding suspected terrorists indefinitely without legal recourse, or should they receive rights of legal due process? Such conflicts, of course, are not exclusively contemporaneous phenomena. History provides abundant evidence of such dilemmas (Lockwood & Harris, 1985).

There is no need to document the plethora of value conflicts that abound throughout the fabric of life and history. No doubt the reader can generate a substantial number of them. The question here is to examine how character education addresses such value issues.

In their theory, contemporary character education advocates do not elaborate on the above philosophical issues related to values. Nor do they acknowledge the importance of engaging students in serious discussion of such matters. Some advocates have even gone so far as to reject such discussion altogether:

> It is ridiculous to believe children are capable of objectively assessing most of the beliefs and values they must absorb as effective adults. . . . Such assessment is largely the responsibility of parents and other appropriate adults. (Wynne, 1985/1986, pp. 8, 9)

So far, in examining character education advocates' theory of values, critics have claimed the advocates have short-changed important questions about the definition of values and the complexities of determining what actions clearly would follow the holding of values. There is another difficulty with their view of values. The advocates fail to address, or apparently even recognize, the pivotal role of principles in interpreting how values should apply in life circumstances. As we will see, without principles a values-based life actually can include immoral actions or commitments.

To illustrate how values can support morally questionable or objectionable behavior, consider the following: American popular culture has long had a fascination with organized crime. The HBO series "The Sopranos" was highly rated. In the recent past, *The Godfather* saga (both the novel and the films) was extraordinarily popular. For the sake of argument, let us assume that these portrayals capture, with some degree of accuracy, what life is like in organized criminal subcultures.

How do values arise in the lives of these organized crime groups? Earlier I identified typical values on many character education lists. Among them are respect, courtesy, obedience, loyalty, honesty, diligence, and courage. Now, are not the members of these groups expected to be respectful, courteous, obedient, and loyal to their bosses? Are they not to be honest in repaying financial or other debts to one another and truthful when incurring them? Are they not to be diligent and courageous when carrying out their crimes? Of course they are. They are expected to act on these values and they are punished most severely, or even killed, if they do not.

My claim that organized crime groups endorse many of the same values as are listed by character education advocates is not just a fictional hypothetical. On November 9, 2007, the Fox news website reported a convicted Mafia leader in Italy had issued a "10 commandments" for mobsters, which listed their rights, duties, and obligations.

This analysis certainly could be applied to other criminal and antisocial groups, organized urban street gangs, for instance. Similarly, I suspect it could be applied to national and international terrorist organizations and many other deviant organized groups. The values of character educators do not belong just to responsible democratic citizens.

Proper moral principles, such as Kant's moral imperative, are what direct values to produce the behaviors that character education advocates mistakenly believe flow directly and automatically from simply holding particular values. For example, a principle such as all people should be treated as one would want oneself to be treated, would attenuate immoral practices based on values held by deviant groups. Values alone do not do the job. It must be clear that the adoption of values such as the ones above does not necessarily direct behavior into prosocial, nondestructive channels. It can do the opposite.

Contemporary character education advocates apparently believe there is consensus on the meaning of value words. We have seen that this is not the case. Interestingly, their failure to carefully examine these issues leads them to a form of philosophical relativism—a position they have firmly, unequivocally rejected! I briefly will show how this happens.

In the absence of principles, values can lead to fundamentally different types of behavior. In the moral/cultural contexts of organized crime or domestic and international terror groups, values can support or lead to behaviors antithetical to the preferences of contemporary character education advocates. Consequently, the behaviors implied or entailed by values are relative. They are relative to the dominant moral conceptions in the societies or social groups with which persons identify.

I am uncertain why contemporary character education advocates do not engage in this more careful analysis and explication of issues raised by values, principles, and social contexts. My guess is they are influenced, in part, by some shared nostalgic view of the supposed good old, tranquil days of presumed moral consensus and social decency.

Contemporary character education advocates do not tell us why their definitions of values and their conclusions of the behaviors that must flow from them should prevail. They simply assert them as moral givens. Assertion, however, is not the same as justification. Why should their view of courage and diligence take precedence over the terrorists' view of courage and diligence? Unless they can argue for it beyond mere assertion or appeal to a particular majoritarian tradition, they are victims of the relativism they vehemently oppose. They do not consider or answer the question of why their societal meanings of these values should be viewed as superior to other societal meanings of these values.

As should other forms of values education, contemporary character education advocates should have sound justifications for their interpretations of the meaning of the values they promulgate and their claims about which behaviors are consistent with them. If someone asks why their value and behavioral claims are correct, in the absence of morally principled considerations, they must fall back on dubious justifications such as: "Well, that's the way it has always been done in our great tradition"; or, "The majority of people in our society believe this way"; or, "Our views are good for you"; or, "We're the experienced grown-ups and we know what's right."

The failure to elaborate on the role and importance of principles in developing an adequate view of values damages seriously the general theory of contemporary character education. A number of the major criticisms of character education stem from this failure. For example, without a satisfactory principled justification of its view of values, contemporary character education rightfully is subject to criticisms that it is arbitrary, is relativistic, ennobles the status quo, or preaches to a congregation already inclined to accept its general position.

In summary, the criticisms of the view of values of contemporary character education advocates are that they:

1. Assume a philosophical tradition of consensus on values
2. Fail to address adequately the meaning of values
3. Do not recognize the debate over the relationship between values and behavior
4. Do not address the issue of degrees of meaning of specific values
5. Do not recognize adequately circumstances in which values may conflict and that single right actions are not easy to come by
6. Do not examine, discuss, or set forth the central role of moral principles in leading a values-informed good life.

THE PSYCHOLOGICAL ASSUMPTIONS

The previous section considered philosophical problems with contemporary character education advocates' discussion of values. In this section I will set out criticisms of their psychological assumptions. These assumptions fall into two categories: (1) assumptions about how values influence behavior, and (2) assumptions about how values are best taught.

Let me make it clear from the outset that I will not be formulating or describing a consensually agreed-upon, research-informed, cogent explication of a clear relationship between values and behavior. There are good reasons for this, mainly that no such relationship has been established. The major criticism of contemporary character education advocates on this count is that they assume that such a relationship exists and that it is simple and direct.

As we know by now, contemporary character education advocates' focus on values is the belief they will lead to good behavior:

> Character consists of *operative values,* values in action. (Lickona, 1991, p. 51, emphasis in original)

> By our definition, "character" involves engaging in morally relevant conduct or words or refraining from certain conduct or words. (Wynne & Walberg, 1985/1986, p. 15)

> Moral *action* is the bottom line. (Ryan, 1989, p. 9, emphasis in original)

I will not belabor the above point. I will, however, show the reader that this alleged connection between values and behavior is far from simple and far from direct. To illustrate this, I will take us on a quick tour of some classic studies, none of which have been contested or overridden by more-recent research.

Ironically, the first major study to show no effects of character education on behavior was conducted by researchers who were supporters of character education. In the early 1920s, Professors Hugh Hartshorne and Mark May (1928) were contracted to design and conduct what became a massive 5-year study. Over 10,000 schoolchildren were subjects in their research.

The most cited finding of the Hartshorne and May research indicated there was no evidence of stable traits of character or clear effects of character education programs:

> The primary finding regarding the nature of character was that children cannot be divided into honest and dishonest categories. It was found that honesty in one situation does not predict well to other situations. In other words, character was found to be situationally specific. (Leming, 1997, p. 34)

Situational variance in behavior has been found in more-recent studies as well. For example, it has been found that people are more likely to help others when the helpers are alone than when they are in groups. Also, people are more likely to help others in subways than in airline terminals (Macaulay & Berkowitz, 1970).

The famed Milgram experiments on obedience to authority also showed situational effects on behavior. In his experiments, subjects were led to believe they were administering increasing dosages of electrical shocks to a "victim" out of sight in another room. An experimenter in a white coat, presumably emblematic of scientific authority, ordered the subjects to continue shocking the victim even after the victim begged for the shocking to cease and then fell silent. Approximately two thirds of the subjects continued to administer shock up to the maximum indicated on the "machine" used to deliver the supposed shock.

In other experiments, Milgram moved the "victims" in closer proximity to the subject and even into physical contact. Closer proximity led many more of the subjects to refuse to continue the shocking regardless of the experimenters' orders. Milgram (1965) concluded, "In certain circumstances, it is not so much the kind of person a man [*sic*] is, as the kind of situation in which he is placed that determines his actions" (p. 72).

I cite these classic studies to show that the behavior of individuals is related, to some degree and in some way, to the circumstances in which the person finds him or herself. We do not know precisely how these situational factors work, but we do know they influence behavior.

The studies cited on situational variation in behavior did not make a systematic effort to determine the values held by the subjects. Perhaps knowing the explicitly professed values of persons will provide better predictors of behavior. In the following paragraphs I will report on some classic studies that attempted to find a relationship between expressed value beliefs and behavior.

In the early 1930s, sociologist Richard T. LaPiere (1970) traveled across the United States with a foreign-born Chinese couple. Surveys and other studies had shown powerful anti-Chinese sentiment throughout the nation. LaPiere expected they would be denied service at hotels and restaurants. To his surprise, out of 251 instances where they sought service, they were denied only once.

After the trip, LaPiere sent a questionnaire to each of the places they had stopped at for service. The questionnaire asked whether the managers would provide service to people of the Chinese race. Over 90% of the respondents said they would not provide service to Chinese patrons! It is difficult to imagine a greater illustration of the discrepancy between professed value beliefs and actual behavior.

Kohlberg (1969) reviewed a number of studies that confirmed the general Hartshorne and May findings of lack of correlation between professions of honesty and actual cheating behavior. "Half a dozen studies show no positive correlation between high school or college students' verbal expression of the value of honesty or the badness of cheating, and actual honesty in experimental situations" (p. 394).

There is also little correlation between people's professed general values and actions they would support. Westie (1965), for example, found that 98% of his subjects agreed that "everyone in America should have equal opportunities to get ahead." However, only 60% said they would be willing to have a Black supervisor on their job. When asked whether they agreed with the statement, "I believe in the principle of brotherhood among men [*sic*]," 94% said they agreed. However, only 29% said they would be willing to invite African Americans to their homes for dinner.

In a comparable study, Prothro and Grigg (1960) found similar discrepancies. There was a high level (94–98%) of agreement with such political value statements as: public officials should be chosen by a majority, every citizen should have an equal chance to influence government policy, and the minority should be free to criticize majority decisions. However, 46% said a legally elected communist should be prevented from taking office, and 63% said no one should be allowed to make speeches against religion.

The Josephson Institute of Ethics, a major character education advocacy group, surveys adolescents on questions of values and behavior. In its 2006 study, substantial numbers of students agreed with general value positions on cheating. For example, 98% agreed that honesty and trust are important in personal relations, 97% said it was important that people trust them, and 83% agreed that "it's not worth it to lie or cheat because it hurts your character" (Josephson, 2006).

In spite of their professed opposition to cheating and lying and their belief in the importance of being trustworthy, 82% of the students said they had lied to their parents, 28% said they had stolen items from stores, and 60% said they had cheated on exams (Josephson, 2006).

These and other studies lead most social scientists to conclude that the relationship between one's values and behavior, and even among one's various values, is erratic, inconsistent, and difficult to predict. This is not to suggest there is no relationship. What is clear, however, is that there is no simple and direct connection. Critics contend that to the extent that contemporary character education advocates claim or imply there is such a direct relationship they are misleading their audience and perhaps themselves (Lockwood, 1993).

Now I will outline criticisms of the values-learning psychology put forth by some contemporary character education advocates. Their views on this subject deserve close scrutiny because if their values-learning psychology is flawed, so will be the teaching methods derived from it.

Before examining their learning psychological assumptions, I wish to take a brief diversion to address a prior question: What values do children hold prior to any formal character education? This is a reasonable question because we should not assume children are devoid of values until they receive some form of values education. Presumably children learn something about what is worthwhile from their families, the media, their religion, and their friends.

There is some reason to believe that children and adolescents profess the same values as those put forward in character education programs. Cross (1997) interviewed 85 elementary, middle, and high school students in an inner-city public school district. Among other things, she asked them what good and bad people are like. They responded as follows:

> Good people are loving, caring, compliant, honest, generous, respectful, kind, nice, helpful, friendly, and disciplined. . . . Bad people, on the other hand, hurt and kill others, drink, lose control, are disrespectful, steal, lie, use drugs, damage property, get into gangs, and commit robberies. (p. 121)

These students' general concepts of good and bad people's values correlate highly with character educators' concepts of the values of peoples with good and bad character.

I do not wish to overgeneralize from Cross's findings. However, I think it reasonable to assume that young people endorse, to some extent, the values listed by character education proponents. This is not surprising because, generally speaking, these values are those of the dominant culture of the United States, if not worldwide. What are we to make of this?

Contemporary character education proponents do not speak to the issue of students already endorsing, in a broad way, the central values of character education. However, I will put words in their mouths that I think they would accept: The values verbally endorsed by young people reflect superficial understandings of what is good and worthwhile. Character education must deepen young people's understanding of and commitment to these values and teach them how to act in accordance with the values.

Let us now turn to the central question of what method or methods of instruction are recommended for use in contemporary character education.

This deceptively simple question has no unequivocally clear answer. Many of the instructional examples presented in the literature of contemporary character education involve classroom discourse. Teachers may preach or exhort. Students may discuss stories in which values are involved and talk about how to act upon them or what they mean. Some schools have a virtue of the week or the month. For example, honesty might be the identified virtue. Teachers then will talk about honesty in various contexts, and there may be school assemblies built around honesty.

Murphy (2002) describes a range of character education programs. Brooks and Kann (1963) also have described a variety of character education programs. More recently, Lickona and Davidson (2005) have described character education programs in high schools. My reading of these programs is that they usually are characterized by classroom discussion and do not rest on any clearly specified learning psychology.

The absence of an explicit learning psychology should not be regarded as a criticism of contemporary character education. Most curriculum and instruction in schools are not derived directly from any specific psychological theory of learning. Whether this is a failing of schooling is debatable. The point is this is not unique to character education programs.

However, if there is an "official" theory of learning endorsed by some contemporary character education advocates, it is behaviorism. Their version of behaviorism stresses rewards and punishments, praise and blame as central in shaping good values and behavior. Wynne (1985/1986) is most explicit about this. Schools that are effective in promoting good character are systematic in employing rewards and punishments. They "managed to provide pupils—both individually and collectively—with many forms of recognition for good conduct," and they are "dedicated to maintaining pupil discipline, via clear, widely disseminated discipline codes that are vigorously enforced and backed up with meaningful sanctions (Wynne, 1989, p. 32).

In *Reclaiming Our Schools*, Wynne and Ryan (1997) write extensively about rewards and punishments. They consider a range of incentives that schools could employ to reward behavioral demonstrations of good character. They also devote an entire chapter to recommendations for discipline policy.

There are a variety of criticisms of their version of behaviorist learning psychology. I will outline three of them here: (1) The rewards that schools have to distribute are few and limited; (2) punishments are ineffective ways of promoting ethical character; and (3) rewards are ineffective ways of promoting ethical character.

One issue with the recommendation that schooling systematically engage in rewards for shaping behavior is that schools' repertoire of rewards is notably sparse. Compared with punishments, schools simply do not have a bulging cache of rewards to distribute. Verbal praise and admirable grades go just so far in shaping behavior and can become useless when overemployed. This may be one reason that Wynne and Ryan fill scores of pages with ideas about school discipline and punishment and a scant few pages on rewards.

Another difficulty concerns whether school rewards are perceived by students as authentically valuable. For some students, receiving gold stars and good grades, having their pictures displayed as being good school citizens, being recognized in an assembly, or generally being praised by teachers and other adults may be seen as worthwhile and gratifying. It is equally the case, however, to find that students, especially adolescents, regard such "rewards" as humiliating or embarrassing and looked down upon by their peers. We know, for example, that the opinions of one's peers are potently motivating and that some peer cultures devalue success in school and disparage whatever accolades schools wish to distribute. Paradoxically, these rewards may be seen as punishments.

Research on the effects of punishment shows that it does not promote good behavior and, perhaps more important, does not extinguish bad behavior:

> The research literature leaves no doubt that punishment is counter-productive. Studies over more than half a century show that when adults use disciplinary approaches variously described as "highly controlling," "power assertive," or just plain punitive, children become more disruptive, aggressive, and hostile. (Kohn, 1993, pp. 167–168)

Another problem critics raise with punishments relates to what young people learn about why they should refrain from doing bad things. I suspect that most thoughtful values educators, including contemporary character education proponents, hope people learn that the reasons for rejecting immoral behaviors are that these behaviors are harmful to the rights and well-being of others—not because we will get punished if caught engaging in them.

Kohn (1993) echoes this point:

> We want children not to do unethical, hurtful things because they know these things are wrong and because they can imagine how such actions will affect other people. Punishment doesn't contribute at all to the development of such concerns; it teaches that if they are caught doing something forbidden, they will have to suffer the consequences. The reason not to be a bully is that someone may punch you back; the reason not to rob a bank is that you may go to jail. The emphasis is on what will happen to *them*. (p. 172, emphasis in original)

Such self-centered reasoning and egocentric calculations are far from the motives we associate with mature moral behavior.

The major criticism of the use of rewards to shape behavior is similar to that relating to punishments. That is, students learn that the "reason" to engage in the advocated behavior is to receive a reward for oneself. There is no intrinsic value, such as doing the right thing for its own sake. Kohn (1993) elaborates a number of other problems with the use of rewards. For example, any behavioral changes associated with rewards are short term and fall away when rewards cease. Rewards also put the recipient in the position of being controlled by another, the individual giving the rewards. This decreases the probability that the rewarded person eventually will develop an autonomous sense of what is right and wrong and engage in behavior precisely because of its inherent moral qualities, not because of the consequences to him- or herself.

Social critics frequently complain about Americans' lack of concern about their communities, a growing disregard for the misfortunes of others, and a strict "look out for number one," bottom-line morality. In many ways, contemporary character education advocates share this view. Ironically, to the extent that their practices promote extrinsic ethical motivations, they may be contributing to the social problems they disdain.

A citizenry reared on the implicit notion that rewards follow from doing the right thing is not to be trusted when rewards, in fact, follow from doing the wrong thing. Take cheating, for example. Persons who cheat, children as well as adults, do so to get a reward. A test cheater is seeking a good grade, which may lead to other rewards, such as parental gifts, school privileges, or access to a desirable university. Adults may cheat to gain money, athletic prowess, and other symbols of social success.

For many American adults, the major rewards of life come from having riches. It is often possible to obtain such wealth through cheating. For example, lawyers are often under pressure to increase their firm's income and by doing so increase their chances of becoming partners. In such circumstances they may bill clients for more time on their cases than actually was spent.

Callahan (2004) documents endemic cheating in virtually all sectors of society. Doctors may receive substantial payments from drug companies for employing untested medications. Auto repair chains may pressure their individual franchises to produce more income, which may be done by charging consumers for unnecessary or phantom repairs. Athletes may use illegal performance-enhancing drugs.

The list of cheating practices is long. From individuals fabricating portions of their income tax returns to giant corporate scandals involving billions of dollars, it has become all too common for persons to illegally and immorally seek the rewards of greater wealth. In many cases the cheaters do not think there is anything wrong with their behavior—other than possibly getting caught. They are simply part of a "moral" system that rewards, often lavishly, certain behaviors.

It may well be that many of these cheaters do not even think about what they are doing in moral terms. In some sense they have been habituated to seek rewards, not to deliberate about their behavior from an ethical point of view.

By no means do I intend to suggest that character education is responsible for widespread unethical behavior in our society. Instead, I offer these examples to show the moral failure of a strict behaviorism intended to promote good character. Both empirically and conceptually, I have come to conclude that behaviorism is an ill-advised psychology for any legitimate program of values education.

There are two other recommended ways in which contemporary character education advocates believe values can be instilled. One of these is modeling, in which students are exposed to significant others who engage in valued behaviors. The second is habituation, the notion that children should practice desired behaviors so that they become, in some sense, second nature. Critics have taken issue with both forms of values instruction.

Contemporary character education advocates frequently portray teachers as powerful figures in students' lives. They contend teachers have the potential to be potent influences in shaping students' character. "Good character also requires obedience to legitimate authority, and teachers are the most prominent extra-family authorities that students meet" (Wynne & Walberg, 1985/1986, p. 16).

Because teachers have presumed legitimacy in the eyes of students and because they wield power, character education proponents believe they should model moral behavior:

> One of the facts of school life is that children watch their teachers to discover how grownups act. While I do not suggest that teachers must be saints, secular or otherwise, I do mean they should be people who take the moral life seriously. Just as teachers should be models of persons using their minds, they should also be seen as models of persons responding to life in a morally admirable way. (Ryan, 1989, p. 10)

The criticism of modeling goes beyond the absence of empirical support for its effectiveness. Consider, for example, the distinction between exhibiting respect for students because as human beings they deserve it, and exhibiting respect for students because teachers want them to emulate the behavior.

In the first case, teachers' respectful behavior is justified because students are to be treated, as Kantian philosophers would say, as ends in themselves. This reflects a moral as opposed to a purely instrumental point of view. In the second case, respectful behavior is intended to teach students to be respectful. In this case, respect is a means to an end. If treating students with respect fails to get them to behave respectfully, there is no justification to so treat them (Davis, 2003).

To emphasize the problem with a means–ends instrumental justification for modeling, consider this extreme hypothetical: Suppose it were discovered that treating students with disdain and disrespect so offended them that it produced a "reverse" psychology. What if students so poorly treated became determined to treat others with respect so they did not suffer the indignities of disrespect? Suppose also that treating them with respect did not promote respectful behavior on their part. If such outcomes were empirically demonstrated, contemporary character education theory would have no grounds for claiming teachers should act in ways that appear respectful as a method for teaching the value of respect.

Another difficulty with teacher modeling is the presumption that students perceive teachers as having legitimate moral authority as opposed to simple power. Students may not hold such a presumption. If students think a teacher is somehow "out-of-it," why would they want to emulate this teacher's behavior or even take seriously his or her moralizing exhortations? A person for whom I have no admiration can model until he or she is breathless and still be unable to influence me in the desired way.

This criticism of modeling is more empirical than conceptual. It is possible that some teachers' modeling and exhortations may be more effective than those of others. Also, peer-oriented adolescents may be less likely than small children to heed their teachers' moral messages. As I indicated, this is a question for empirical research rather than philosophy. There is, however, some survey evidence that students do not perceive their teachers as moral authorities (Lockwood, 1993).

Contemporary character educator advocates regularly emphasize the role of habit in establishing preferred values and the behaviors believed associated with them. They frequently cite Aristotle as the classic philosopher in this camp. When asked how to teach virtue, Aristotle claimed you do it by having people practice virtuous behavior (Wynne & Ryan, 1997). One becomes honest by learning to behave honestly, courageous by doing brave acts, and so on.

Ryan (1989) stresses the role of habit as critical to effective character education:

> Once learned, certain moral competencies must be habituated. Moral actions, such as telling the truth when a comfortable lie is handy or saying the right but unpopular thing when silence is easy, need to be practiced responses. One cannot

stop and weigh consequences every time a moral event arises. Moral actions must be practiced, habituated responses to life situations. (p. 10)

There are a variety of criticisms of this notion of engendering right habits. For one, how do we know what habits to have students exercise? Take honesty, for example. We might agree that, as a general rule, it is good to be honest. But certainly there are situations in which honesty must give way to other values, such as courtesy. For example, suppose your favorite aunt asks if you like her new hat. You think it is ugly but, for the sake of courtesy, you say it is quite attractive. My earlier discussion of values and behaviors shows that determining what actions follow from specific values is not a simple matter. It becomes increasingly complex in situations where values are in conflict.

On this count alone, the promotion of habits is on shaky ground. Do contemporary character education advocates claim to have some "Encyclopedia of Morally Right Answers" that tells us the morally correct thing to do in all situations? They certainly make no such claim, but it remains unclear how they would determine what actions to habituate.

Although they cite Aristotle as promoting virtuous habits, they fail to discuss his arguments for the promotion of reason. Reason is not the whole cloth of the moral life, but it is a central part of it. If habits are to be shaped, they should lead to thoughtfulness in moral matters. Aristotles's views on this, ignored by contemporary character education advocates, have been summarized by Peters (1967) as the paradox of moral education: "The palace of reason has to be entered by the courtyard of habit" (p. 214). Critics say contemporary character education appears to wish to keep students in the courtyard (Lockwood, 1985/1986).

THE EDUCATIONAL PERSPECTIVE

The final criticism of contemporary character education advocates transcends my two general categories of criticisms of theory and criticisms of their assumptions about values learning. This criticism will be outlined briefly here and developed more fully in subsequent chapters.

In short, neither the theory, assumptions about learning, nor recommended practices of contemporary character education advocates are informed by any well-considered, research-based conception of human development. This is a serious failing. Even the most casual observers of schooling know there are important differences between young children and adolescents. These differences are not merely physical; they have to do with views of the world, education, and personal responsibility, for instance.

Contemporary character education proponents know that there are differences between elementary-age children and high school adolescents. Nonetheless, their character education goals, teacher roles, and instructional strategies do not take these differences into account in any systematic fashion. Some published character education materials target students at different ages and grade levels. The distinctions that inform the construction of these materials, however, seem more intuitive than systematic and research-based. Certainly they get no guidance from contemporary character education advocates.

There is no easy answer to the developmental lacunae in contemporary character education. This is especially surprising given that both Lickona (1976) and Ryan (1981) were well steeped in and early supporters of moral development theory and research. Both published in this field. For whatever reasons, they virtually abandoned their immersion in this rich tradition when formulating their conceptions of contemporary character education.

One, admittedly simplistic explanation for the absence of a systematic developmental concept behind contemporary character education, especially in its formative years, is that most of the work was done in the elementary grades. Except for recently, the large majority of examples of character education practices in the literature came from elementary schools. Perhaps this intense focus on young children led to less-thorough thinking about adolescents or, worse, to a belief that what was appropriate in character education for young children was also appropriate for adolescents.

For whatever reasons, contemporary character education advocates do not speak in depth about developmental matters, nor is their work clearly informed by any coherent concept of human development. One of the purposes of this book is to bring a developmental perspective to the theory and practice of contemporary character education. This is done in the hope that developmentalism can inform a worthwhile view of character education, strengthen its theory, and enhance its practice.

SUMMARY

In this chapter I summarized critiques of contemporary character education. They were categorized under criticisms of the general theory, the psychological assumptions, and the absence of a developmental perspective.

The general theory of contemporary character education was criticized for a number of reasons:

1. The bleak view of human nature
2. The emphasis on personal responsibility for bad behavior to the exclusion of social, political, and economic factors
3. The unwarranted assertion of historical and contemporary consensus on the nature of values and their transmission
4. The narrow belief that individual possession of particular values will solve social problems
5. The mistaken belief that desirable values clearly lead to particular desirable actions
6. The failure to take seriously circumstances in which values come into conflict with one another
7. The failure to recognize that moral principles, not simple assertions of values, are critical in determining moral behavior

The psychological assumptions also were critiqued for a number of reasons:

1. They give the impression of a simple, clear, and direct relationship between values and behavior when there is none
2. They give the erroneous impression that children do not already hold, at least verbally, the values that character education intends to promote
3. To the extent that they endorse a philosophy of learning, it is the inappropriate and inadequate one of behaviorism
4. Their emphasis on teachers modeling desired behavior in order to promote such behavior among young people is limited and ill-considered
5. The suggestion that children be taught to habitually engage in specified behaviors is misconceived

The final general criticism of contemporary character education is its failure to take seriously developmental differences between young children and adolescents. This failure is seen as a major flaw in the theory and a damaging blow to the overall success of those purposes of character education that are worthwhile.

Chapter 3

Responses to the Criticisms

In the previous chapter I described a variety of criticisms of contemporary character education proponents' general theory and of their psychological bases. This was done with an eye to modifying relevant features of the theory and psychology of contemporary character education as a response to *sound* criticisms. To me, and probably to most readers, this seems like an eminently reasonable thing to do. After all, if we are shown where we are in error, does it not make sense to correct that error? Surely most reasonable people would say, yes. Oddly enough, this most mature and sensible response to *thoughtful* criticism is rare in the field of values education, if not education in general.

I will not speculate on why the notion of program improvement through critical dialogue remains more of an academic ideal than a practical reality. I will, however, offer a few views on the general issue. Later I will address criticisms specific to contemporary character education and assess which of the historical and current criticisms have merit.

HOW TO RESPOND

Previously I intentionally have referred to *sound and thoughtful* criticisms. It is these types of criticisms that deserve response. I am not speaking of harsh, politically motivated, mean-spirited, or ideological posturing forms of criticism often designed more to forward the critic's agenda than to take seriously the positive purposes of criticism. I deliberately have chosen an analytic approach to the criticisms introduced earlier in order to foster the kind of dialogue that will lead to improvements in the theory and practice of contemporary character education.

There are a variety of ways of responding to criticisms: (1) One can ignore them and fail to respond; (2) one can respond and argue that the central points of the critics are not well taken; or (3) one can weigh carefully the criticisms and respond in a balanced manner by modifying one's position where appropriate. This chapter will reflect the objective, balanced approach.

Contemporary character education advocates have yet to make a systematic response to the many criticisms outlined in the previous chapter. These criticisms, carefully argued some years ago, are still relevant and deserving of attention. To the extent advocates have responded, they have argued that the critics either misunderstand character education or their criticisms are unfounded (Benninga & Wynne, 1998; Lickona, 1998). To date, the advocates' reaction to criticism has embodied the second type of response mentioned above. By and large they have acknowledged but discounted the criticisms (Lickona, 1998).

The third response to criticism is to assess the soundness of the critics' assertions and respond to them as appropriate. If the criticisms are seen as missing the point, that should be explained. On the other hand, if the criticisms are sound, they should be acknowledged and, where appropriate and possible, should inform modifications of the theory and practice of contemporary character education. The question then becomes, how do we determine the soundness of criticisms? Sound criticism need not be considered true or irrefutable, but the quality of the criticism should merit its being taken seriously and assessed for its applicability to the practice under consideration.

ASSESSING THE SOUNDNESS OF CURRICULAR CRITICISM

For purposes of this section, I will attempt to take the stance of an impartial judge. My task is to set out general criteria for assessing the soundness of criticisms of any educational program. To facilitate this assessment, I have set out the following major questions to consider when weighing the soundness of a criticism.

Are the Critics' Attributions of the Advocate's Position Accurate?

Critics must characterize the positions of advocates in order to target their criticisms. Otherwise they would have nothing to criticize, nor would we know what they were talking about. For example, a critic might contend that an advocate's program would require teachers to engage in actions for which they are neither trained nor qualified. To make such a criticism sound, the critic must, at a minimum, accurately describe the teachers' role put forward in the advocate's program. If the critic's characterization of the teachers' role, as set forth by the advocate, is accurate, the criticism may be sound.

Is the Criticism Derived from Sound Theory, Research, or Practice?

This question is directed at what might be called the inherent substance of the critic's basis for criticism. The critic may have characterized accurately some feature of the advocate's program, but the criticism brought to bear on that feature may not be derived from sound theory or research.

To reiterate, this criterion for assessing critical validity looks at the grounding of the critic's stance, not at the accuracy with which the advocate's program is portrayed. If the critic's theory or research grounding is flawed, then so is the criticism. This does not, however, mean the target curriculum is worthwhile or beyond other criticisms.

To What Extent Can the Criticism Lead to Reasonable Modifications of the Advocated Program's Theory or Practice?

It should be clear by now that answering these critical assessment questions is not hard science. The answers are not absolute and require us to bring to bear both scholarly judgment and equanimity.

Substantive criticism should carry with it clear implications for changes in programs' theory or practice. The implication here is that criticism should be practical or useful in some fashion. Some critics may reject this notion and view criticism as an end in itself—serving as a demonstration of alternative paradigms or profound political differences. For my purposes here, however, I will stipulate that sound curricular criticism shows us, or implies clearly, ways in which the targeted program's theory and practice can be changed and improved upon.

The requirement that sound criticism give direction to some feature of program modification is based on an ameliorative notion that the purpose of critical dialogue is to advance the quality of the theory, research, or practice of whatever is being appraised. This does not mean that the modifications suggested by criticism are automatically reasonable or should be followed. It does mean that a necessary quality of sound criticism is that it shows us how the critic wishes to modify or, conceivably, eliminate the practice.

There are any number of responses an advocate might make to sound criticism, and I will not attempt to exhaust them here. I am asserting strongly, however, that developing responses should be a matter of sincere, professional judgment in which criticisms are examined openly rather than defensively and that responses should be made carefully and rationally. This is the ideal I will try to embody as I assess the criticisms of contemporary character education.

RESPONDING TO CRITICISMS OF THE GENERAL THEORY

In this section I will assess the criticisms leveled against contemporary character education advocates. The organization of the criticisms employed in the previous chapter will provide the structure for this section. I will assess the criticisms and consider both their soundness and the extent to which they should lead to modifications of the general theory or psychology of the advocates. If modifications are warranted, I will suggest what they might be. In later chapters I will incorporate these into a fuller explication of my position on how contemporary character education should be formulated.

I am hopeful that contemporary character education advocates will respond to these criticisms as well. Whether these responses are endorsed by the advocates or not, they will form part of the basis of the rationale for character education that I set out in later chapters.

The View of Human Nature

One criticism of contemporary character education advocates is that they have a *pessimistic view of human nature*. This suggests that humans are inherently barbaric and must be firmly controlled lest civil society be ripped apart. Some advocates indicate they share this view of human nature (Benninga & Wynne, 1998; Wynne, 1985/1986).

According to this criticism, the bleak view of human nature leads character education advocates to favor stringent means of controlling the behavior of youth. In addition, it leads them to a highly conservative political stance emphasizing social stability and maintenance of the status quo. Some also believe this view leads the advocates to overemphasize individual responsibility for social ills and to downplay or ignore the impact of social, economic, and political inequities.

By and large, the criticism that character education advocates hold a pessimistic view of human nature accurately reflects their view and is sound on that count. How to respond to this criticism, however, is problematic. It is not easy to determine what the criticism presumably entails. For example, does holding a pessimistic view of human nature logically require one to believe that deviant individuals are responsible for social ills, that stringent behavioral controls are necessary, and that a conservative political/social agenda must be served?

Contemporary character education advocates do emphasize personal responsibility and favor some forms of behavioral control. Is this necessarily because they share a grim view of human nature? I am inclined to say that people who favor behavioral control, personal responsibility, and a conservative social agenda need not share an identical view of human nature. That is, one can arrive at one or more of these conclusions on other grounds.

Holding a particular view of human nature may be *implied* by one's educational agenda, but the agenda is not *entailed* by the view. For example, one can believe that some degree of government is necessary for managing human affairs, without explicitly endorsing any particular view of human nature.

I might add that it is by no means clear how one could demonstrate that human nature is one thing or another. Debating the true nature of human beings may be of great interest to many but, at best, it is only marginally relevant to the enterprise of contemporary character education.

Given the uncertainty as to what a grim view of human nature entails for character education, I am inclined to respond as I have above. Essentially, my assertion is that the key components of character education theory may be loosely consistent with some view of human nature, but they are not derived directly from such a view nor are they entailed by a particular view.

Let us now turn to two additional but related criticisms of the general theory. These are that contemporary character education advocates downplay or *ignore the effects of political, social, and economic influences on negative behavior* and *emphasize personal responsibility for negative behavior.*

The general theory says virtually nothing about the impact of societal influences on behavior. The advocates do not elaborate their views on social theory. This criticism is based more on what they do not say about societal effects than on what they do say. Clearly, however, they do emphasize the need for personal responsibility. The focus of their version of character education is to instill values in individuals with the expectation that these values will direct behavior. As a result, I regard these two related criticisms as sound.

Although these criticisms may be well taken, I am not at all clear on how best to respond. At its most extreme, the environmental view might suggest we put our efforts into social, political, and economic activism and abandon character education. There are a variety of reasons to reject this view, not the least of which is that the efficacy of all forms of education is constrained by social contexts; this is not unique to character education. I have not heard the critics suggest abandoning all educational efforts. That our activities are constrained and goals imperfectly met is not, in itself, cause to give up the effort.

It is obvious that our educational work does not occur in an environmental vacuum. The outcomes of our efforts are invariably a result of our programs' interaction with the social, political, and economic context in which they occur. While this is obvious, it is not clear precisely how this interaction works. Critics do not show us how specific environmental factors influence the workings of our character education programs and affect their outcomes.

Based on the previous discussion, I would respond to the critics who contend that contemporary character education ignores the social, political, and economic forces that influence the behavior of young people by agreeing that such forces are at work. In addition, I would say acknowledging that such forces are in play is one thing, but such recognition does not inform us as to how they directly affect our efforts. Character education, as do other forms of education, must attempt to influence individuals within their social context, not in spite of it.

The criticism that contemporary character education advocates overemphasize individual responsibility is consistent with the environmental criticism. Whether character education programs overemphasize personal responsibility is a matter of judgment. They certainly do emphasize it. Because the vast majority of the advocates' discussions and recommendations are directed toward influencing the values and behavior of youth, this criticism is well founded.

The best response to this criticism is to acknowledge that character education does focus on affecting individuals, as do other instructional programs in schools. I would not respond to the claim that this emphasis is excessive until the critics spell out more of what they mean by this. I would acknowledge, however, that the success of our programs will be tempered by the societal context in which our students, and their teachers, live and act. That is a given reality, and there is not much we can do about it.

The View of Values

A number of questions have been raised over contemporary character education advocates' view of values. Advocates have been criticized because:

1. They claim there is a social and historical consensus on what values are worthwhile
2. They bypass issues related to the definitions of values
3. They imply it is easy to determine what behaviors are consistent with specific values
4. They fail to take seriously the reality of value conflicts
5. They do not recognize the pivotal role of principles in guiding the morally good life

I will address each of these in order.

Critics have taken issue with character education advocates' claims of *historical and social consensus on value issues.* As mentioned earlier, Wynne

(1985/1986) asserts that there is a "great tradition" of consensus on moral values and the need to instill them in the young. Also, throughout the writings of advocates, essentially the same list of values is brought forth as reflective of a broad social consensus. We may conclude that the critics accurately have portrayed the views of the advocates and that the criticisms have merit.

For me, the best response to the critics' assertion that there is no historical consensus on value issues is to agree. This should not be surprising because I am one who has raised this criticism. I would, however, suggest that while moral philosophers have disagreed powerfully on any number of values-related matters, there is general agreement that moral issues are important and deserving of careful analysis. The classic works of John Stuart Mill and Immanuel Kant illustrate this. Both of them carefully explicate the importance of moral issues and analyze them at length. Here there is consensus. Their views on ideal moral principles reflect a distinct lack of consensus. Mill's focus on consequences of actions as determinants of right action stands in direct contract to Kant's view that it is the nature of the act that determines its rightness, not the consequences.

Critics generally agree that there may be a social consensus on what general values are worthwhile. When asked to make a list of important values, diverse groups of people will generate lists that are remarkably similar (Gee & Quick, 1997). To the critics, however, these lists reflect merely a consensus on abstract, unspecified, honorific labels. After all, who would be opposed to honesty, courtesy, respectfulness, and so on? Contemporary character education advocates appear to believe that this consensus is more than superficial agreement on nice-sounding words and carries deeper and relatively uncontroversial meaning. It is here that critics take issue with the advocates' notion of social consensus on values.

I will take this opportunity to comment on consensus. Why is it that advocates wish to assert an historical or contemporary consensus on important value issues? I believe they think that the existence of consensus strengthens their justification for character education. For some observers it probably does. We should remember, however, that consensus means merely that most people currently think something or historically have thought something. Does this mean that what they think or have thought is justified? The answer is a resounding "No!" It is easy, if painful, to show there are worldwide historical examples of oppression by groups in power over the powerless. We also can point to recent social consensus that women may not vote or be allowed to own property. Consensus, historical or otherwise, cannot substitute ethically or logically for careful reasoning about right and wrong.

Another critical concern about contemporary character education advocates is their *apparent belief that the meaning of values is easy to come by.* Their writings suggest that determining the definition and full meaning of values is not problematic. Critics have portrayed this stance of character educators accurately so the criticism has substance.

In considering this criticism, it is useful to note that some ethical philosophers refer to our obligations to uphold general values as our *prima facie* duties. In essence this means we should follow these values *all things being equal.* The problem, of course, is that all things are rarely equal. For example, asserting honesty as a value does not tell us when to be honest, what to be honest about, how fully honest we should be, or, in the face of conflicting values in a specific situation, whether we should be honest at all. These matters need to be examined in context. This does not mean that honesty is not a good thing; it does mean that simply endorsing it gets us only so far in determining what we should do.

Contemporary character education advocates should acknowledge that this criticism is well taken and respond in at least two ways. First, when they are prescribing specific behaviors, they should spell out the context in which these behaviors are appropriate and explain to students why they have identified the prescribed behaviors as warranted. This will help us understand how they reason through these serious moral matters and, more important, show that their prescriptions are not arbitrary, politically motivated, or idiosyncratic. Second, especially for older students, their curriculum should allow students to engage in deliberations addressing endorsed the value of honesty within academic and applied contexts.

A related criticism is that contemporary character education advocates suggest that *the relationship between values and behavior is relatively simple and direct,* downplaying issues related to determining what behaviors are consistent with what values and also assuming a unproblematic psychological relationship between values and behavior.

Both philosophical and psychological scholarship shows there is no simple or direct relationship between general values and behaviors (Kamtekar, 2004). Contemporary character education advocates should accept these outcomes of research. There are times, of course, when the relationship between values and behavior is conceptually clear and we should not ignore that. For example, all things being equal, armed robbery is wrong. On the other hand, much of the complex moral life requires persons to think through situations and determine what right actions are called for. Character education curriculum and instruction must not ignore this brute fact of the moral life in both its theory and practice.

Critics also have contended that contemporary character education advocates *downplay or ignore issues related to value conflicts*. These issues are pivotal, as was discussed in Chapter 2, to the difficult moral decisions we face, typically those in which values come into conflict. Advocates are certainly aware of the potential for value conflicts but they do not discuss them in any depth. This criticism correctly describes the advocates' writings and therefore is sound.

In responding to this criticism, advocates should acknowledge the tough moral reality that values frequently come into conflict in situations requiring difficult decisions. These conflicts are one thing that makes these decisions difficult. I am uncertain what else to recommend as a response for the advocates because they have not, nor need they, set out a detailed curriculum for K–12 character education.

If the advocates had proposed a clear K–12 curriculum, they might have responded to this criticism in a substantive fashion by claiming that value conflict issues could be discussed in the higher grades. Elementary school students essentially would be taught central value concepts, such as honesty and respect, and how they should be acted upon in relatively simple situations. A developmental perspective could be brought to bear on the timing for addressing various value issues with students. We do not, of course, know what the advocates would do or whether my response would be satisfactory for them.

To reiterate, the previous point is not intended to suggest that Lickona and the other advocates should set out a curriculum. What they have done is to present a general rationale and argument for the kinds of activities and programs they believe would embody the central precepts of their view of good character education. This is a worthwhile task. My suggested response makes sense only if they wish to be specific about what they recommend for different grade levels. In later chapters I hope to show how this may be done.

A final criticism of the advocates' view of values is their *failure to take seriously the role of principles* in the making of sound moral decisions. Throughout most of their writings, contemporary character education advocates give the impression that obedience to a prescribed list of values will yield a citizenry that does the right thing when confronted by choices involving values. For the advocates, it is the values that are highlighted, but the principles that would guide how they should be applied are ignored. As a result, the criticism has merit.

Contemporary character education advocates' failure to engage in reflection and discussion of the pivotal role of principles in guiding moral behavior is perplexing. As was shown in Chapter 2, adherence to simple values can characterize "right" behavior and thought in criminal subcultures as well as in the good society envisioned by the advocates.

In a criminal culture, obedience to legitimate authority may mean murdering someone at the direction of your mob boss or bombing a civilian building at the direction of your terrorist leader. In a criminal culture, honesty may mean informing on a member of your group who is leaking information to the police or other government officials. Contemporary character education advocates may well consider this a twisted enactment of moral values—as do I. The question is, why are these enactments wrong? Simply asserting that they are, is an inadequate rationale. Moral principles must be brought to bear to show how values should be acted upon.

I suggest that the best response to this would be for contemporary character education advocates to explain what principles guide their judgment of the conceptual and behavioral meanings of their listed values. This would be a first step in recognizing the crucial role of principles in moral decision making and action.

There is a second response that advocates may wish to make. That is to explain how students might be engaged in analysis and discussion of what would demonstrate sound principles (Simon, 2001). The central question for examination would be, in effect, what moral generalizations should guide us in deciding the meaning of values and what actions should be taken with regard to them. For me, this is a vital part of sound character education. Later I intend to show both why and how this investigation can be pursued with our students.

The Final Criticism

The final criticism of contemporary character education set out in Chapter 2 was its *lack of a developmental perspective* in its curricular thinking. Throughout their work, the advocates do not offer any systematic explication of the developmental differences between young children and adolescents. In part as a consequence of this, the advocates do not outline how character education's curriculum and instruction would be conceptualized and organized differently for young children compared with adolescents. Therefore, this final criticism has merit. This is a fundamental and significant oversight that must be addressed for character education to be fully justified.

The best response to this general criticism is for the advocates to agree both that they have not set out a developmental perspective and that one is needed. Conceding that this criticism is well taken does not undermine the essential aims of contemporary character education. The assumption of the developmentalist is that the goals of any K–12 plan of instruction will be better realized if the plan takes into account developmental differences.

To say that developmental considerations should be taken seriously does not fully inform the process of curriculum design. Of course we all know by experience or intuition that older students are different in significant ways from young children. This widely accepted assumption does not give us any guidance for designing curriculum and instruction. We need to know what differences are relevant for creating effective instruction. For example, we need to know how abilities and interests vary across age groups if we wish to avoid instruction that infantilizes adolescents or frustrates elementary school children by being beyond their current developmental constraints. There are other contributions that a well-established developmental perspective can provide; these will be discussed in greater detail in the next chapter.

SUMMARY

This chapter has offered suggested responses to the more prominent criticisms summarized in Chapter 2. There I spelled out a variety of criticisms made of contemporary character education advocates. These criticisms were directed primarily at the proposed general theory of contemporary character education and its psychological assumptions as put forth by the advocates.

In this chapter I have argued that well-taken criticisms deserve a serious, more substantive response from the advocates. I proposed some criteria for what constitutes such sound, well-taken criticism. These criteria were applied to the criticisms to determine which ones deserved a response.

Having identified sound criticisms, I proceeded to suggest what could serve as sound responses to them from advocates. These, of course, are suggestions to be accepted or rejected by the advocates as they see fit, but I hope they will be taken seriously.

It is my view that sound criticisms deserve thoughtful consideration by the advocates of any program being examined. These criticisms could lead to sound changes in the theory and rationale for a program. They also could lead to changes in the practices recommended by program advocates. The remainder of this book contains my observations and suggestions to modify and strengthen the current conception of contemporary character education based on responses to these criticisms as well as other factors.

Chapter 4

The Formation of a
Developmental Perspective

This chapter may appear to be a rather lengthy digression from what has come before. I trust, however, that the reader will see that it is a vital bridge from what has been to what is to come.

WHY WE NEED A DEVELOPMENTAL PERSPECTIVE

One of the critical absences in the work of contemporary character education advocates is their lack of a developmental perspective. Implicitly and explicitly they wish character education to be, at a minimum, a K–12 program. What is missing, however, is the application and framework of the well-researched science of human development. Character education is not just to be for young children or for adolescents. Given the dramatic changes as children grow, any and all proposed character education programs should address these changes appropriately. Developmental differences in students interact with curriculum and instruction and, in part, determine how students interpret instruction and what they learn from it.

It must be emphasized at the outset that my intent here is to promote the use of developmental concepts and research findings for character education's mission; it is not to have developmental psychology use character education for its purposes. In the latter case, one would be arguing that character education should serve to promote some preferred version of healthy psychological development, such as advancing stages of moral reasoning. This may be a valuable educational aim, but it is a different argument. Here we are examining what developmental psychology can contribute to character education.

By using developmental psychology for the purposes of character education I mean that psychological theories and research findings should inform the process of curriculum design for the realization of age-appropriate character education goals. In some cases these findings may lead us to refine or redefine these goals. We also may find that the promotion of development is consistent with the goals of character education. In no case, however, do I argue that the promotion of development should replace or supersede the primary goals of character education.

The application of developmental knowledge to character education may irritate some developmental psychologists and educators. For one thing, I will be borrowing from developmental schemes in an eclectic, general, and relatively uncritical way. I will not be explicating these psychologies in detail nor will I be assessing scholarly critiques of them. I am convinced that the broad outlines of these systems are well established and have utility for addressing some of the limitations of contemporary character education. My intent is to show how knowledge from the field of developmental psychology may aid in the formulation of more effective character education programs.

The hope is that character education theorists and curriculum designers will select whatever versions of developmental psychology they find most warranted and persuasive and use them in ways similar to what I will be describing. There are a variety of developmental concepts in the field of psychology that may inform the process of character education, and what follows is not intended as a comprehensive listing of them.

The working assumption here is that we need a general understanding of key differences between children of different ages and developmental stages. These conceptions not only must be descriptive of those differences but should yield guidance for shaping curriculum and instruction in character education across the school grades.

I am using words such as "broad" and "general" intentionally when referring to the ideas to be taken from the developmental psychologies. This is because developmental schemes necessarily create generalities about persons at different phases of development. The schemes do not, nor could they, fully and specifically explicate the characteristics of any individual at any phase of development. The described differences are generalities, and the guidance they will give us for curriculum and instruction also will be general. This, of course, does not mean that their conceptions are without merit or their curricular guidance without value. If these generalities yield useful modifications of character education theory and practice, more precise features of developmental psychology can be brought to bear to further enhance character education.

A sound developmental perspective potentially can help us with curriculum and instruction in a number of ways. I say potentially because these psychologies are formulated to help us understand human development; they are not designed directly to guide educational practice. Nonetheless, these psychologies can help educators in the following ways:

1. They may provide help in determining what topics and issues are likely to be important or unimportant to students at different grade levels. This can help us ascertain what content is likely to be engaging to students. It also may help us avoid content that students will see as irrelevant, incomprehensible, or unimportant. Job-related value issues, for example, would have little meaning to elementary-age students but could be engaging for adolescents. Unless curriculum and instruction are engaging, understandable, and seen as relevant by students, their desired impact may be limited.

2. They may help us know what intellectual abilities students are likely to have or not have at different points in development. This can aid us in setting instructional tasks that are challenging to students but not beyond their capabilities.

3. They may provide direction in predicting what attitudes toward, or understandings of, moral and other values are pervasive at different stages. This can help us identify what responses students are likely to have to our lessons and aid in planning for how to deal with these responses most effectively.

AN OVERVIEW OF DEVELOPMENTAL PERSPECTIVES

Developmental psychology is an enormous and rich field of study. As a consequence, selecting which developmental perspectives to mine for guidance in character education is daunting. My primary criteria for choosing these perspectives are that they should speak to the three potential uses of developmental psychology outlined above, they should describe age-specific functional and cognitive abilities of school-age children at all levels, and they should contribute to our characterizations of developmental differences in how young children and adolescents deal with value issues.

To the best of my knowledge, what I am doing here has not been done before and is, consequently, an untested enterprise. Because of this, I want to increase the probability that the major outlines of the theories and research to be employed are well established. To try to ensure this, I should use psychologies that are well known in the academic community and that have been subjected to extensive scholarly research and critical dialogue. It would not be a fair test of the curricular utility of developmental perspectives to employ one or more schemes that have not been subjected to rigorous scholarly examination.

Virtually any principles of developmental psychology can provide some insight for character education. While Carol Gilligan's (1982) elegant explication of the human development of caring and responsibility orientations was not intended to inform educational practice, there are educational implications from her research. For example, the educational views of Nel Noddings (2002) have been partly informed by Gilligan's observations.

For my purposes I want developmental psychologies that offer very broad, even grand, claims about the differences between children and adolescents. I believe these psychologies have the greatest potential for providing developmental insights that best help us reconstruct character education. My choices should, by no means, suggest that I dismiss the potential value of other developmental psychologies.

Given the guidelines suggested earlier, I have decided to assess the possible contribution to character education of two major and venerable developmental schemes. The first, from the psychoanalytic tradition, is that of Erik Erikson (1963). Erikson postulated a sequence of life stages from birth to old age, but may be best known for his insights into the psychology of adolescence. The second, from the cognitive-developmental tradition, is the moral development work of Jean Piaget (1965, 1970) and Lawrence Kohlberg (1969, 1970, 1980). I conflate these two because Piaget formulated some of the key principles of this tradition and Kohlberg expanded on Piaget's work.

In the following sections I will describe these developmental psychologies. Then I will set out possible contributions these works can yield for the theory and practice of character education.

ERIK ERIKSON'S DEVELOPMENTALISM

Erikson was born on June 15, 1902, in Frankfurt, Germany. His father left soon after he was born and his mother remarried a man named Homberger. Young Erik Homberger did not take to schooling and drifted around Europe intending to become an artist. In Vienna he met Anna Freud and became interested in psychoanalysis. He pursued a certificate in psychoanalysis and, as part of his education, underwent psychoanalysis by Anna Freud. He came to the United States in 1933 and began the practice of child psychiatry in Boston. When he became a citizen in 1939, he changed his last name to Erikson. He taught at various universities across the nation and finished his career at Harvard University. He died in 1994.

Erikson is no doubt the pre-eminent psychoanalytic developmentalist of the 20th century. While he adhered to some key Freudian theories, Erikson moved well beyond the sexuality-driven developmentalism of Freud and incorporated precepts from social theory, history, and anthropology to enhance his life stages developmental theory.

While Erikson may be best known for his insights into adolescence and for coining the phrase "identity crisis" to depict the psychosocial struggles of that trying time, his stages describe pivotal developmental tasks from birth to old age. According to Erikson (1963), each person encounters these stages and the central life challenges they present. The tasks at each stage are described as polar extremes. The individual must cope with these polar tensions and resolve them in a relatively positive manner. The effectiveness of this coping and resolution colors each individual's identity development, adjustment to future-stage issues, and challenges of life in general.

Erickson's Stages

Briefly, Erikson describes his eight stages as follows:

1. *Trust vs. Mistrust.* In the first years of life, the child depends for his or her physical and other modes of well-being on others and must trust his or her needs will be met. If these needs are not met, the child may develop an unhealthy mistrust of others.
2. *Autonomy vs. Shame and Doubt.* In this stage the toddler begins to do things for him- or herself—walk, talk, and explore the environment. Ideally, in this stage the child begins to develop a sense of confidence in his or her ability to manipulate and control the environment. If parents or caretakers discourage or rebuke such behavior, excessive self-doubt or a sense of shame may be the unhealthy outcome.
3. *Initiative vs. Guilt.* In this stage the preschooler begins to engage in self-directed and -initiated play and uses imagination to create or envision little adventures. The child must be taught certain limits, given his or her energy levels, but these limits must not be so severely enforced as to produce a maladaptive sense of guilt for wrongdoing.
4. *Industry vs. Inferiority.* The primary grades to the beginning of middle school encompass this stage, in which the child must adjust to the world of schoolwork, with its attendant expectations for teamwork, cooperation, and competence, and develop relationships with nonfamily members. Work must be done systematically, according to adult direction with standards imposed by others, and it is evaluated in some form. If accomplishments are ignored or treated harshly or unfairly by others, the child may develop a pervasive sense of incompetence and inadequacy.
5. *Identity vs. Role Confusion.* According to Erikson, this developmental stage is the central theme of adolescence. The pivotal challenge at

this stage is to develop a robust sense of self—to know who one is and how one may fit well into society. The adolescent is in transition from childhood to adulthood, and coping with the many changes and challenges that this entails. If this crisis is not resolved in a healthy way, the individual loses a strong self-concept, can become self- and socially destructive, and may affiliate with marginal, antisocial groups and organizations.

6. *Intimacy vs. Isolation.* This is the central stage for young adulthood. Having successfully navigated earlier stages, the individual now is confronted with coping with the tension between making and sustaining commitments to others while maintaining a sense of self. Failure to develop the capacity for mature affiliations can lead one to an unhealthy feeling of isolation.

7. *Generativity vs. Stagnation.* This is the stage of middle adulthood. Here the individual is concerned with serving future generations through his or her own children, work productivity, and creativity. Failure to adequately deal with this crisis can lead to failure to care for others or be a contributing member of society.

8. *Ego Integrity vs. Despair.* In this final life stage, the individual comes to terms with his or her life. In a way it involves taking stock of the choices one has made and the successes and failures of one's life. This helps prepare one, in a psychologically healthy way, for the end of life. Failure to properly adjust to this stage can lead to preoccupation with past negativities, a focus on poor decisions, and a general sense that one has not led life in a fruitful manner.

These eight stages cover, according to Erikson, the total life span. Stages 1 through 5 are most relevant to our considerations for character education in schools.

These stages provide a depiction of central issues in personal development and a general explanation of what constitutes psychologically healthy development through the life span. In his writings Erikson shows how the treatment of persons from infancy onward affects the way they resolve the tensions of each bipolar stage. Healthy personality development, not surprisingly, falls somewhere between the extremes.

The stages, as a map providing directives for improved mental health, are not necessary for purposes of refining character education. The point is not to use character education to further some Eriksonian conception of psychological well-being. Rather, Erikson's work might better be used to inform us about making character education more effective and engaging to young people. Although Erikson did not intend his work to directly shape educational practice, his concepts and insights are rich enough to provide some guidance for developmental character education.

The Implications for Character Education

For character education, the stages can be understood as pervasive concerns with which children and adolescents cope over time as they deal with their environment in and out of school. Erikson's work has a number of implications for character education. The following listing offers the rationale for how Erikson's work can shape character education's theory and practice.

1. In one sense, character education can be seen as identity education. Erikson's understanding of identity is that it is constructed from the individual's interactive relationship with others and society. This dynamic reciprocity shapes who we are. If character education is understood as an effort to shape a fuller, better integrated moral being, then desirable moral identity is clearly a primary goal of character education. We want people to behave in morally responsible ways and to contribute to improving the quality of society.

Morality should and must be an integral part of one's being. The central question of identity is, "Who am I?" A full answer to this question will include some characterization of the self as a moral being. Am I what I should be? What principles shape my relationships with others and shape me as a member of society? What guides me in making critical ethical decisions that affect my life and the lives of others? These are questions that lie at the heart of both Erikson's theories and character education.

It is useful to think of our work as character educators as helping form and shape the identity of young people. This needs to become part of the rationale for contemporary character education as well as a guiding purpose for instruction. As part of the rationale, it moves us from a narrow focus on shaping behavior to a larger vision of participating in shaping persons. As part of instruction, it reminds us to have students consciously reflect on how the content of our curriculum "fits" with their emerging concepts of who they are and who they wish to be.

2. Later developmental stages are enmeshed with issues that younger children are unlikely to find deeply and personally engaging. For example, character education curriculum and instruction that emphasize what elementary-age students should do to prepare for a productive life in society are likely to be found developmentally inappropriate. Engaging students in serious assessments

of what constitutes a fulfilling career, how one might relate to coworkers and bosses, or how best to influence governmental agencies is best left for adolescent years, at the earliest. Children's letters to members of Congress are often cute, but it is doubtful they have any significant impact on students' enduring beliefs about responsible citizenship.

3. Erikson's concept of issues of identity and the development of the self in adolescence is, of course, much fuller than what is outlined here. There is also more to adolescence and the earlier stages than what he describes. Nonetheless, his views can give some general direction for character education.

The adolescent struggle for positive identity is in large part a battle against the negativity of role confusion—floating, ill-formed notions of possible selves, none of which are fully integrated or coherent. As a bulwark against fears of a hopelessly diffused identity, adolescents may identify worshipfully with clique leaders or celebrities. They can become clannish and focus on clothing, special jargon, and other external signs of their in-group versus out-groups. Adolescents are particularly vulnerable to the sway of espoused religious or political ideologies and their charismatic leaders who are believed to supply life meaning against uncertainty (Erikson, 1963).

These features of adolescence do not require that particular topics be included in or excluded from character education curricula. They do, however, imply some caveats for values education practices for adolescents.

Adolescents often become deeply absorbed in themselves as they wrestle with the task of establishing a sound identity. For each of them, the questioning of life, roles, and values feels like a novel experience. The adolescent may not imagine that others, especially adults, have ever thought deeply about anything of substance. For some, this can lead to a disdain for adult value authority because it presumably has not grown from hard, intense, critical thought.

Contemporary character education supporters wish to get young people to hold a particular set of values and value judgments and to engage in specific values-related behaviors. Such directive efforts may be relatively successful with early elementary school children but will face hard going with most adolescents engaged in forming their own identity, not mirroring some adult preferences. A colleague of mine, who was evaluating a values education program, vividly recalls focus groups of adolescents telling him: "We don't want teachers telling us to be moral. We know what's right and wrong."

Adult efforts to mold adolescents into persons with a specific moral identity, particularly if those efforts are indoctrinative or perceived as such, face stiff competition from other objects of adolescent identity affinity. Erikson's work shows that such antipathy to adult moral exhortations is not a simple matter of rejecting adult authority. For one thing, there are other sources of messages that capture adolescent attention. Also, according to Erikson (1963), "The adolescent mind is essentially a mind of the *moratorium*, a psychosocial stage between childhood and adulthood, and between the morality learned by the child, and the ethics to be developed by the adult" (pp. 262–263).

These observations might lead one to forsake any systematic moral education efforts with adolescents. Such a conclusion would be hasty and, arguably, profoundly wrong-headed. What should be abandoned are didactic modes of instruction intended to promulgate some particular set of moral positions valued by adults. What should not be abandoned are appropriate efforts to engage adolescents in serious deliberations about morality. Such deliberations should be entered into with the intent of adult involvement in helping form moral identities rather than forcing moral identity into a specific template.

Later chapters will speak more about Eriksonian implications for character education curriculum and instruction. Here it is stressed that adolescent character education should deal with emerging moral identity struggles, not try to preempt them with some adult-preferred outcomes. It is critical that we find ways to responsibly and productively influence the development of moral identity. It will be argued that failure to do so contributes to social and interpersonal moral bankruptcy.

4. Cooperative learning frequently is recommended by contemporary character education advocates. How cooperative groups should be created and instructed can be informed by Erikson's stages. From elementary to middle school, for example, it seems especially important that students in groups be taught how to interact in ways that emphasize how to be trusting of one another (Trust vs. Mistrust) and that all members be allowed to suggest purposes for activities or interpret what the teacher has assigned (Autonomy vs. Shame and Doubt, and Industry vs. Inferiority). Of Industry vs. Inferiority, Erikson notes:

> This is socially a most decisive stage: since industry involves doing things beside and with others, a first sense of division of labor and of differential opportunity, that is, a sense of the *technological ethos* of a culture develops at this time. (p. 260, emphasis in original)

For younger children the teacher may pay somewhat less attention to cliques when assigning cooperative groups. For early and late adolescents, however, the formation of identify often is powerfully connected to their in-

and out-groups (Identity vs. Role Confusion). Creating productive cooperative groups requires that this be taken into account. At a minimum, teachers
should make and enforce very clear rules governing what behavior counts as
cooperative and what does not. The point is to minimize peer tensions and
promote a focus on the group task.

The teacher must evaluate and grade cooperative-group work carefully.
Erikson's stages suggest that younger children's evaluations should include effort (autonomy, initiative, and industry). These qualities are presumably, if
subconsciously, important and rewarding to younger students. Theoretically,
the behaviors identified as examples of autonomy, initiative, and industry promote children's sense that school life is relevant to their lives, not alien to them.
Such investment in schooling and character education curriculum design and
instruction increases the chances for program effectiveness.

For adolescents, not only should grading consider how well they worked
together as a group but also, and perhaps more important, grading strategy
should assess carefully the individual's performance in contributing to the
group product. The adolescent may feel closely affiliated with his or her peers,
but the formation of healthy adult moral character requires recognition of the
responsibilities of autonomous individuality, not simple group allegiance. Also,
principled morality transcends mere conformity to group norms, and character education should promote this central component of moral identity.

This sketch of Eriksonian contributions to the practice of character education is not intended to be exhaustive. Instead, I hope the reader will generate
other applications. In Chapter 6 I provide more illustrations of how developmental perspectives can inform the practice of character education.

LAWRENCE KOHLBERG'S EXPANSION OF DEVELOPMENTALISM

This section sets out the major features of cognitive-moral developmental psychology and considers what may be gleaned from it in the service of
character education. It begins with a brief discussion of Jean Piaget. This is
because Piaget, although only tangentially interested in moral development,
established important principles of developmental psychology upon which
Kohlberg expanded a great deal.

Piaget's Influence

Piaget was born in Switzerland in 1896. During his childhood he became
interested in biology and was involved in nature clubs. While in high school he

published, in professional journals, his research on mollusks. He also became interested in philosophy, and by the time he finished his doctoral dissertation at the age of 22 he had published both articles and a related novel.

Upon turning his attention to psychology, he moved to Paris to work with Theodore Simon on intelligence testing. Piaget became intrigued with why children gave wrong answers to questions and what these revealed about the way children thought. He returned to Geneva and, as his research continued, established that children's thinking was significantly and structurally different from that of adults.

One of the central premises of Piaget's work is that the development of cognitive structures in the individual is not a consequence of what people are directly taught or "read" from the environment. Instead, the changes occur as the individual interacts with problems in his or her environment. When current structures of thought are perceived intuitively as inadequate to deal with any given cognitive challenge, more adequate and sophisticated structures emerge over time.

It is critical to note that these structural changes are a consequence of active interaction with issues, scientific and other, that the individual faces in the environment. In effect, the individual makes meaning that solves these problems. Development of these cognitive structures is a dynamic achievement and does not occur automatically or through formal instruction.

Piaget's (1965) study of cognitive development led to the formulation of stages. He showed how people moved cognitively from the scientifically inadequate stage of sensorimotor operations to higher forms of thought, called formal operations, that enabled abstract scientific and mathematical thinking.

The development of thinking about morality also found a place in Piaget's wide-ranging studies. On this topic he found that moral thinking also progressed through stages. He identified two general stages: the stage of heteronomous moral thought and the stage of autonomous moral thought.

At the stage of heteronomous moral thought, the source of children's notions of right and wrong lies outside of the self. Morality is, in effect, in things outside of personal judgment. The rules of a game, for example, are believed to be somehow built into the game and not a human construction. Similarly, lying is bad because the act is bad in itself; it is not bad because of its consequences to human relationships.

Piaget found that the stage of autonomous moral thought emerged by the teen years. At this stage, individuals recognize that morality is a human construction and can be evaluated according to its effects on persons and human relationships. The wrongness of lying, for example, is now judged immoral because of its violation of mutual respect among persons.

Kohlberg's Beginnings

The American psychologist Lawrence Kohlberg was intrigued by Piaget's work on moral development. Kohlberg was born in Bronxville, New York, in 1927. After attending Andover Academy, he spent time smuggling refugee Jews from Europe into Israel. In 1948 he enrolled at the University of Chicago, where he remained for his graduate work in which he focused on moral development. In 1968, he moved to Harvard University, where his research continued and his interest in educational practices designed to promote moral development blossomed. He died in 1987.

Kohlberg built upon Piaget's research, detailing moral development from childhood to adulthood. In the process he extensively elaborated stages in moral development. Over the years, Kohlberg's name has become synonymous worldwide with ground-breaking theory and research on the psychology of morality.

Kohlberg's Stages of Moral Development

Like Piaget, Kohlberg was interested in characterizing the thinking that children and adolescents brought to problem situations. The problem situations that Kohlberg presented to his subjects were moral dilemmas. Moral dilemmas are stories in which a character must confront a necessary, but difficult, decision involving conflicts with moral values such as life, liberty, property, truth telling, and so forth. The subject is asked whether the character made the right decision (or what decision should be made) and, more important, to give reasons to support the judgment of right and wrong.

Kohlberg employed a number of dilemmas, but the most cited and prototypical was the Heinz story. As described in Chapter 1, Heinz was unable to raise enough money to buy an expensive drug that might save his dying wife. The local druggist would not reduce the price and Heinz broke into the store and stole the drug. Subjects were asked whether what Heinz did was right or wrong and to give reasons for their judgments.

The reasons given in various dilemmas had strong similarities within individual subjects but substantive differences across age groups. Kohlberg called these clusters of similarity *stages*. For example, at approximately 10 to 12 years of age, children often considered self-interest to be the key "principle" in resolving moral problems. That is, what was right was what got the central character that which was in his or her best material interest. For example, one child might say that Heinz should steal the drug because he needed his wife to help around the house. Another child might say that

Heinz should not steal the drug because he might get caught and have to spend a lot of time in jail.

In the previous example, the two children disagreed on whether Heinz should steal the drug, but they both agreed on the general way in which the solution should be reached. For both of them, the right decision was that which squared with a calculation of what was in Heinz's self-interest. They differed, of course, in their calculation of self-interest in this situation. In later years, their orientation to self-interest would give way to different predominant considerations, such as the quality of the relationship between husband and wife, what laws applied, or what human rights should be protected when addressing the dilemma.

These stages of moral reasoning evolved over time. The self-interest stage common to young children eroded as the primary right-making consideration and was replaced by other factors. Kohlberg found that the stages of moral development followed the same sequence in each person. For all, the earlier focus on self-interest was replaced by a concern for the well-being of members of the family or primary group. For some, this was later replaced by a general concern with society and its laws.

Discovering and tracing the development of stages of moral reasoning was the centerpiece of Kohlberg's work. Originally he posited six stages of moral development. Later on, following further conceptual and empirical analyses, he questioned the developmental status of his sixth stage. In the following summary of the stages I include the sixth stage as a distinct moral/philosophical orientation, which it is. The reader should not assume, however, that this stage follows sequentially from Stage 5. That is an empirical question whose answer has not been established.

Kohlberg divided his stages into three categories. The first two stages of reasoning he called preconventional. The third and fourth he called conventional. The fifth and sixth stages he called principled or postconventional. Kohlberg's (1980) original stages of moral reasoning are briefly described as follows:

Preconventional Stages

1. *The punishment and obedience orientation.* Here the physical consequences of an action determine its goodness or badness regardless of the intention of the actor. If one breaks a dish, it is wrong even if it was an accident while one was helping clean. Also at this stage, deference to power and avoidance of punishment are central values. Adult figures are right because they are strong and hold positions of authority.

2. *The instrumental–relativist orientation.* As mentioned above in the discussion of the Heinz case, what is right at this stage is determined by what meets the material interests of the actor. There is also a simple sense of reciprocity in that one may believe he or she owes something to another if the other has given something to the person in the past. In this case, moral obligation becomes the equivalent of returning a favor.

Conventional Stages

3. *The "good boy–"nice girl" orientation.* Rightness is associated with what is traditionally good behavior in one's group. Goodness consists of helping others and receiving approval according to customary practices. Good intentions are especially important in determining right behavior.
4. *The maintenance of law and order orientation.* Rightness is associated with obedience to law and rules, and the maintenance of social order. Doing legal duty and respecting official authority are important components of right decisions.

Principled or Postconventional Stages

5. *The social contract orientation.* Rightness typically is associated with personal rights that have been agreed upon by society. Within this context, the U.S. Constitution, for example, may be understood to be a social contract, as opposed to a body of statutory law. Such contracts are not unwavering and can be renegotiated so that human rights are better protected if unjustly threatened.
6. *The universal ethical principle orientation.* Right is defined by conscience in accord with abstract ethical principles that should guarantee justice for all persons regardless of their position in society. Such principles derive from respect for human dignity.

The reader will note that this description of stages, as with Erikson's, is abbreviated. More detailed descriptions are available elsewhere (Kohlberg, 1971). Two other caveats are warranted: (1) Identification of a subject's primary stage of moral reasoning is determined through an elaborate stage-coding system of extensive interview transcripts. The simple, general descriptions above are not used, nor should they be, as the sole basis for stage scoring. (2) The stages characterize the reasons people give as *part* of their making of judgments of moral rightness and wrongness. As such, the stages characterize only a portion of an individual's makeup. The stages are not personality types.

The responses of two subjects illustrate some of the major features of moral stages. The two subjects are both male high school seniors who have just read the Heinz dilemma and are being asked whether what Heinz did was right or wrong.

> *Subject A:* "I don't think he should have stolen it because he'll probably get in trouble. [When asked whether letting someone die is worse than stealing:] I think stealing would be the worst. You could always be accused of stealing, where you couldn't help it if she dies so you couldn't be blamed for it. And you could get over it a lot easier than stealing where it would be totally on your criminal record."

This reasoning most clearly reflects a Stage 2 orientation to the dilemma.

> *Subject B:* "As I see it there are two moral laws in conflict here—there's the law not to steal and the law or principle of life. To me, his wife's right to life, not because she's his wife but because she's another person, is more important than the law against stealing or the druggist's property rights. I think the right to life is the most basic right because all other rights are dependent upon it."

Subject B's reasoning reflects the principled level of moral reasoning.

These two excerpts from high school classmates illustrate several points about the stages. Most notably, age and stage are not synonymous. These boys are the same age and obviously are employing different forms of reasoning. Their reasoning also shows how different stages construct the issues in a dilemma. For Subject A, the effects of the decision on Heinz's life are pivotal considerations. For Subject B, balancing conflicting rights in a situation takes precedence over other factors such as self-interest, Heinz's feelings for his wife, and the law.

Psychological Properties of the Stages

Extensive research on the stages of moral development have led to a number of findings.

1. *Development to the highest stages is rare.* Few people attain Kohlberg's level of principled moral reasoning. Unlike Erikson's stages, which we all

encounter at relevant phases of life, most adult moral development ceases at Stages 3 or 4.

2. *The stages are cognitive, not affective.* Kohlberg's stages are ways of thinking about moral right and wrong. They are not stages of feeling or emotion. This is not to say that one does not feel strongly about his or her moral points of view. The stages, however, reflect forms of concepts and thought about moral issues. This is why his system is called cognitive-developmental.

3. *Development follows an invariant sequence.* Stage development is sequential. Stage 1 is followed by Stage 2 is followed by Stage 3, and so on. People do not skip stages or regress to previous stages.

4. *Interaction with the environment influences development.* As with Piaget's cognitive development, moral development is a consequence of a person's interactions and experience. The stages represent more philosophically sound ways of dealing with the moral issues that that person encounters. That is, in effect, higher stages represent more morally satisfactory resolutions of ethical issues than do lower stages.

5. *Instructional practices can stimulate stage advance.* Educational interventions that engage students in discussion of real or fictional moral dilemmas promote greater moral development among those students compared with those who do not have the experience (Blatt & Kohlberg, 1971). However, these gains are modest and, as a general rule, do not promote development to the principled level (Leming, 1997).

6. *People rarely reason exclusively at one stage.* Subjects virtually never use the same stage of reasoning for all dilemmas they discuss. They typically do employ a dominant (50% of their reasoning or higher) stage in their reasoning, with a lesser percentage of adjacent stages appearing as well.

7. *Subjects intuitively prefer reasoning at stages higher than their own and reject lower stage reasoning.* When presented with a variety of samples of moral reasoning and asked which is best, subjects select reasons above their own dominant stage. Conversely, when asked to identify poor reasons, subjects identify reasons below their dominant stage.

8. *People have difficulty understanding reasoning at stages higher than their own but no difficulty understanding reasoning at lower stages.* When tested for

comprehension of a variety of reasons, subjects had difficulty grasping the content of reasoning above their dominant stage. On the other hand, they had no difficulty understanding the content of reasoning lower than their own.

9. *Moral reasoning is a partial predictor of moral action.* Knowledge of an individual's stage of moral reasoning does not provide a direct prediction of what action he or she will take in a concrete situation. Moral reasoning is connected with moral action in complex ways that are not fully understood (Gielen, 1991).

There is a philosophical distinction between moral judgment and moral deliberation. Moral judgment occurs when we are determining the rightness or wrongness of an action that has been taken. Moral deliberation occurs when we are deciding what we should do in a particular situation. Kohlberg's stages are derived from studying subjects' moral judgments, not their deliberations.

10. *Moral development involves the growth of perspective taking.* Advanced stages of moral reasoning presume, both logically and psychologically, expansion of one's ability to understand the points of view of known other persons as well as abstract notions of society and its members' needs (Kohlberg, 1976). The cognitive ability to understand the perspective of others, their thoughts, interests, and feelings, also follows a developmental pattern. This form of development has been studied carefully by Robert Selman (2003).

Selman identified four general levels of social perspective taking. By early elementary grades children have moved from the egocentric perspectives of preschool days to an understanding that others may have different perspectives from their own. By high school years adolescents can understand their own perspectives and multiple perspectives of others.

11. *People do not always reason at the highest stages of which they are capable.* The predominant stage of reasoning obtained from the Kohlberg interview on his fictional moral dilemmas may be understood as the highest reasoning stage of which a person is capable; it represents one's ceiling capacity for moral reasoning in Kohlbergian terms. In making real-life moral judgments, a person may or may not employ the highest stage of reasoning of which he or she is capable. Lower stages of reasoning may be employed in a specific situation. This reflects the standard distinction between competence and performance in other realms. That is, for various reasons, people do not always perform to the upper limit of their cognitive capacity.

12. *Moral stage development occurs across cultures.* Kohlberg (1969) reported that cross-cultural research findings suggest that his stages of reasoning (at least up to Stage 4) occur in non-Western as well as Western populations. As a result he claimed his stages were culturally universal.

Philosophical Characteristics of Kohlberg's Stages

As we have seen, Kohlberg's developmental psychology is far-reaching and bold. Perhaps as striking as his psychological claims are his philosophical claims. Kohlberg argued that the moral reasoning of the later or higher stages was philosophically better than that of the earlier or lower stages. Higher stage reasoning represents more sound, preferred ways of making moral judgments (Kohlberg, 1973).

The fact that a stage emerges later than other stages does not, in itself, make it preferable. Consider Erikson's stages, for example. The Integrity vs. Despair stage comes later in time than the Generativity vs. Stagnation stage. The later appearance of the former stage in no way suggests that it is better than the earlier. It is just later.

To claim that higher stages are better just because they come later in a sequence is to commit a logical error. Philosophers call this the naturalistic fallacy. The nature of the error is to presume that because we have seen the way things are, we also have seen the way they should be. To support the claim of the moral superiority of higher stages requires a philosophical argument of why they are to be preferred, not just a psychological claim that higher comes later (Kohlberg, 1971).

Kohlberg's argument is drawn from certain premises in secular moral philosophy. Among other things, moral philosophy attempts to define the characteristics of a "good" moral stance. That is, what criteria best help us identify sound moral points of view? These premises lead to a formulation of the ideal features of a preferable ethical point of view. Among the characteristics of such a moral stance are:

1. Impartiality—we want our ethical principles to be fair for all, not to favor one person or group over another.
2. Human Dignity—we want our ethical principles to derive from a respect for the worth of human beings.
3. Human Rights—we want our ethical principles to define and consider fundamental human rights.
4. Universality—we want our ethical principles to be consistent in similar situations, not generating one judgment in one situation and a different one in a similar situation.

Principled moral reasoning carried with it these preferred meta-ethical characteristics. Earlier stages did not. Consequently, Kohlberg concluded that the higher stages of reasoning were morally superior ways of making judgments than were the lower stages.

There is a simpler, less philosophically abstract way to determine what modes of moral reasoning are better than others. This way appeals to our considered intuitions. Imagine that someone is going to make a moral judgment about some action that you have taken. At the lowest stages, that individual might think only about what's in his or her own self-interest. If the person thought only of his or her self-interest, you would feel your interests had not been fully or fairly considered. If the person thought only about what was right or wrong in his or her primary group, you would feel your case was not fairly considered if you were not a member of that group. If the person only thought about what law might apply, you might justly feel your case was not properly considered if the law was unfair or unclear, or if no law relevant to the case had been passed.

The considerations rejected in the previous paragraph all reflect lower, nonprincipled stages of moral reasoning. If I were the object of judgment, I clearly would prefer the judge to employ principled reasoning that took my legitimate rights into account rather than the considerations that dominate lower stage reasoning. This preference for principled reasoning is more intuitive or "common moral sense" than the careful ratiocinations of meta-ethics. Both ways of thinking, however, support the notion that principled moral reasoning is a more satisfactory, preferred, and adequate way of making moral judgments.

Before leaving this discussion of moral philosophy, two clarifications need to be made. First, Kohlberg's argument is *not* that principled moral reasoning automatically leads to an easy, clear, and defensible final judgment. In some situations, two well-meaning people employing principled reasoning may differ as to what judgment is entailed by the principles. Second, there is an assumption that one can be moral without being religious. Principled moral reasoning does not presume any particular religious conviction or necessitate any spiritual doctrine. Religion is neither rejected nor required for the higher, more considered moral life.

Kohlbergian Contributions to Character Education

The cognitive-developmental tradition of moral psychology, best represented by Piaget and Kohlberg, has a number of implications for contemporary character education in both theory and practice. This volume cannot exhaust all possible contributions from this vast body of work. Nonetheless, identified below are several points that have particular bearing on our thinking about character education.

1. Contemporary character education should include the promotion of principled moral reasoning as part of its rationale and mission. It appears that some character education advocates may be interested only in ensuring that the behavior of young people is nondestructive and socially positive. We also have seen that some advocates believe a behavioral approach should be employed to shape this behavior. In Chapter 2 I argued that both of these propositions are flawed, both philosophically and psychologically.

Character education advocates need to accept that while the promotion of morally responsible behavior is a central goal of the movement, such behavior must flow from sound moral thinking and not from the mechanical application of some version of behavioral psychology. This is illustrated potently in *A Clockwork Orange*. In this novel, Anthony Burgess (1962) spins a futuristic tale in which criminals are powerfully conditioned to become ill whenever contemplating violent behavior. His gripping story portrays the moral emptiness, as well as impracticality, of such a program of behavior shaping.

The promotion of sound moral reasoning should become part of the fabric of contemporary character education theory and practice. In Chapters 2 and 3 I showed that neither the application of behavioral psychology nor the inculcation of particular values can foster civic decency. Our citizenry must be capable of and prone to employ sophisticated, principled, and autonomous moral thought. There is no "Encyclopedia of Morally Right Behavior for All Situations," nor is there a behavioral conditioning program to ensure that such behavior will persist when external rewards cease.

2. Character education teachers, especially those holding well-thought out, carefully considered moral points of view, may be surprised by the moral assertions of students—especially children. I have known teachers who were shocked by the statements of some of their young students. For example, some students might say that it is morally right to give a bully whatever he wants because he is strong. The Stage 2 selfishness orientation is often particularly distressing.

Cognitive–moral developmental psychology teaches us that the thinking of children often is dramatically different from that of adults, and that development to higher levels of thinking is a slow process. This knowledge can inform our instruction in at least two ways. First, by understanding how children's thinking may be at significant variance from that of adults, we can maintain professional composure as we solicit their views in discussion of values-related issues. Second, awareness of the dynamics of development can help us productively, positively, and appropriately challenge immature thinking without engaging in fruitless, invariably ineffective lectures about how children should be thinking.

3. Although the reasoning about right and wrong that students bring to moral dilemmas varies by age and stage, virtually all find moral issues engaging. True dilemmas are perplexing and attract our interest and concern. Even early elementary-age children can recognize that there is something at stake in ethical issues and assert their views on what counts as a fair solution to a problem.

Character education curriculum should provide students the opportunity to discuss ethical issues. These may be in the form of fictional or true events. Many elementary character education curricula use children's literature. These stories raise value issues, and students may be asked to identify the problem faced by the characters, to state what the characters felt, and to describe how they made their decisions. To ensure that students have the chance to consider the moral issues in a story, they should be asked to explain the reasons for their judgments of right and wrong in the stories. Not just what did a character think and do, but was the decision right or wrong and why?

Good literature, for both children and adolescents, provides a wealth of situations in which characters face moral issues. There are also, of course, many moral issues that arise in the life of schools, in history, and in current events. These too can become part of the curriculum and be discussed and debated by students. As with all good moral development instruction, students should be urged to explain, defend, and debate the reasons they use for their judgments—not simply assert them. This is critical, as is providing students with an assortment of reasons and arguments to consider so that they can test out their ideas in fair and open discourse. The general instructional strategy, of course, is not to try to gain class consensus, but to consider and evaluate a range of reasons and opinions. In the long run, this practice advances maturity of moral thought.

4. Both perspective taking and empathy are important related capacities for moral development as well as for other aims of character education. Perspective taking refers to the ability to understand how others perceive a situation. This also follows a developmental pattern. Immature perspective takers assume that others see the world in the same way that they do. Mature perspective takers can recognize, with minimal distortion, how others view situations (Selman, 2003).

Empathy is the capacity to experience the feelings that others are experiencing. This too has developmental features. Children mistakenly think often that others' feelings are the same as theirs. Persons with mature empathetic capacities can experience the feelings of others even when they are different from their own (Hoffman, 2000).

For ordinary instructional purposes, it is not necessary to make fine distinctions between perspective taking and empathy. They both can be treated as what is known prosaically as "putting yourself in another's shoes." Proficiency with this capacity permits us to make more sound value judgments because it allows us not only to better understand others but also to more accurately grasp the consequences of different actions or policies. Consideration of consequences is, after all, a vital feature of informed and well-justified decision making.

5. Both contemporary character education advocates and moral development scholars argue that ethical relativism is an unacceptable moral point of view. In short, extreme relativism is the view that moral judgments cannot be proven right or wrong and therefore all are equally valid. Moral developmental theory and research have notable implications for handling this issue in character education curriculum and instruction.

Put most simply, the response of contemporary character education advocates to ethical relativism is not only to reject it, but emphatically to show students the difference between right and wrong and to teach them to believe, appreciate, and act on the basis of what their teachers say is right and wrong. This frequently leads to instruction intended to fill students with knowledge of right and wrong behavior according to the curriculum designers. Such instruction can be seen as indoctrination, even if subtle.

Moral development research shows that indoctrination is ineffective and that progress toward mature morality is a result of experiences, including formal instruction, in which students must grapple with moral issues as they formulate their own autonomous moral points of view. The most straightforward implication of this is that character education should abandon, or at least minimize, top-down preaching of what is right and wrong and, instead, engage students in serious, responsible deliberations about moral issues.

SUMMARY

The impetus for this book derives from the belief that contemporary character education has failed to incorporate a developmental perspective in its advocated theory and practice. As a result, we lack a systematic way to make informed, thoughtful decisions as to what modes of character education curriculum and instruction are likely to be most effective for different levels of students. The informed conclusion is that instruction will be most successful if it "fits" with key features of students' developmental status.

In this chapter I identified two major, comprehensive developmental psychologies with an eye to assessing what contributions they might make to our thinking about contemporary character education and the strategies that would enhance its impact. After summarizing the scholarship of Erikson and Kohlberg, I speculated on how the core propositions from their work could guide us in reformulating contemporary character education to strengthen its theory and practice.

Forthcoming chapters will recast the theory and practice of character education to take into account sound criticisms discussed earlier and implications from developmental psychology outlined in this chapter. What is to come is not a specific body of recommended curricular materials and practices, but a framework to help shape our thinking and select our materials and practices in ways I will argue are both more defensible and more effective.

Chapter 5

The Theory of Developmental Character Education

In this chapter I will lay out the theory of developmental character education. Subsequently, I will show how pedagogical practices can be informed by a developmental viewpoint.

In previous chapters, the status of contemporary character education, as conceived of by its leading advocates, has been presented and assessed regarding its strengths and weaknesses. This assessment required an explication of criticisms of contemporary education, with an eye toward improving the effectiveness and relevance of practice. I claimed that some criticisms lacked curricular significance but that others were sound and deserved to be incorporated into any revision of the theory and practice of contemporary character education.

In addition, I observed that a chief shortcoming of contemporary character education advocates is their failure to incorporate a developmental perspective into their theory and practice. Put another way, contemporary character education advocates do not adequately or systematically distinguish how their practices should differ when teaching children of disparate ages.

The intent of all of these considerations is to establish a well-justified stance from which to transform the theory and practice of contemporary character education.

A MODIFICATION OF THE DEFINITION OF CONTEMPORARY CHARACTER EDUCATION

Earlier, in Chapter 1, I bemoaned the ambiguity of what is meant by character education. In essence, many teachers claim to be engaged in the practice of character education but there is no consensus as to what it is and what it isn't. This lack of definitional clarity and consensus creates problems for teachers, program evaluators, policymakers, and the general public.

In the absence of widespread professional agreement on such a definition for contemporary character education, a survey of the literature on contemporary character education advocates allowed me to infer a definition by examining the major tenets they champion as well as the features of values education approaches that they reject. From this process I generated the following working definition of contemporary character education:

Character education is any school-initiated program designed to shape directly and systematically the behavior of young people by teaching explicitly the nonrelativistic values believed to directly induce socially acceptable behavior.

This definition effectively captures contemporary character education advocates' focus on directly molding the behavior of youth by teaching them socially endorsed values. Arguments and analyses in previous chapters questioned the presumed direct connection between certain values and behaviors and contended that, for a variety of reasons, character education should concentrate on promoting particular forms of students' moral and values-related thinking about themselves and others.

The above refocusing of contemporary character education, with the vital addition of a developmental perspective, yields the following definition of developmental character education:

Developmental character education is any school-initiated program designed to shape the moral and value understandings and commitments of young people in ways that positively influence their behaviors and engender ethically worthwhile relationships with others and society. The curriculum and instruction of these programs explicitly take into account significant developmental differences between young children and adolescents.

The definition of developmental character education shows in a general way how it modifies and reshapes contemporary character education. In what is to come I elaborate on developmental character education so that the reader can understand more fully its meaning, justification, and preferred practices.

It should be clear by now that developmental character education is not intended to totally replace contemporary character education. It is, however, a substantive revision of it and includes the incorporation of developmentally derived components. I accept many aspects of contemporary character education, such as the notion that schooling must involve some modes of values education and that the promotion of civic instruction be part of that education. Given the substance of past chapters, I trust the reader will know more fully where developmental character education is consonant with contemporary character education and where it departs from it.

THE GOALS OF DEVELOPMENTAL CHARACTER EDUCATION

Unlike climbing Mount Everest or winning a basketball championship, the goals of developmental character education, like virtually all worthwhile educational aspirations, are never met fully and precisely. In endeavoring to shape thought and behavior, we never accomplish our aims with 100% success or certainty.

> The goal of developmental character education is to foster rich understandings and assessments of value-related issues in human interaction, to appreciate and recognize the critical importance of morality, and to promote autonomous virtuous behavior consistent with sound ethical principles.

The first part of the goal speaks of understanding values-related issues in human interactions. Here the aim is to promote students' ability to recognize values, contemplate them, make judgments about them, and examine how they arise in various situations. This is part of helping students understand and analyze the moral dimensions of interacting with others and being a member of society.

The rich understanding dimension of the goal includes promoting the ability to grasp the viewpoint of others. Students need to understand how other persons perceive situations, what needs and expectations they have, and how they are likely to be affected by different actions. This perspective taking focuses not simply on the perspective of another individual but also on the perspectives of "generalized others," such as social groups and society at large.

The values comprehension feature of the general goal is also related to the behavioral component. The assumption is that we cannot expect people to behave in ethically responsible ways if they do not perceive how values are involved in a situation. This is a minimum first step in doing the right thing. We cannot expect one to try to do what is morally right unless he or she recognizes that the situation calls for moral thought and action.

The goal also refers to making assessments of values-related issues. Students are taught not only to recognize value issues when they arise in situations but also to evaluate the rightness or wrongness, goodness or badness of value meanings and decisions. Ultimately we want our fellow citizens to make sound judgments when the rights and well-being of themselves and others are at stake. Making ethically correct decisions is not robotic behavior or mindlessly conditioned obedience to the dictates of some presumed moral authority. This making of value judgments is an active, vital human enterprise and needs to be informed by careful thought and the application of well-grounded principles.

Appreciation of the importance of morality is another component of the goal. We want students not only to understand and evaluate various aspects of morality but also to recognize its importance to us all. We want students to admire those who do the right thing, to be motivated to do the right thing, and to be proud of how they answer such fundamental questions as: Why should I do what is morally right?

The final element of the goal speaks of promoting autonomous virtuous behavior. This is to stress that developmental character education is concerned with the present and future behavior of students, not just their ability to think and talk intelligently about values-related matters.

The concept of autonomous behavior should be emphasized. The theory of morality in this approach rejects the view that the essence of morality is compliance with the dictates of some designated moral authority. As argued earlier, true moral thought and behavior in the face of difficult situations is a consequence of careful reflection on complex considerations.

The general goal of developmental character education and its subsequent elaboration stated above highlights key properties of the approach. There is an emphasis on influencing behavior through nurturing students' understandings of value issues and obligations rather than by employing behavioral conditioning or demanding obedience to some moral authority. This focus is more likely to promote sound ethical behavior in novel and/or stressful situations.

FEATURES OF DEVELOPMENTAL CHARACTER EDUCATION

The elaborated goal statement provides some understanding of developmental character education. Fuller attributes of the approach are clarified by seeing how developmental character education is not susceptible to the substantive criticisms of contemporary character education set out in Chapter 2. To facilitate this explication, I will convert the criticisms into key questions and provide the developmental character education responses.

To what extent does developmental character education view values-related negative behavior as a consequence of political, social, and economic forces as opposed to personal choice derived from holding improper values? Developmental character education advocates recognize that values-related behavior is not simply a matter of individual choice occurring in an environmental vacuum. Both common sense and social science research acknowledge that value-related behavior is a consequence of complex contextual and personal factors that interact in concrete situations that present alternative choices for resolution. Personal values influence behavior, but are not the sole determining factor.

We know that personal values do not, in themselves, directly determine behavior. Knowing a person's values does not predict his or her behavior in any given specific situation. The converse is also true. That is, our observations of behavior do not tell us directly what value motivations are reflected in the actions. To illustrate with an extreme example, imagine you see a teenaged boy assisting an elderly woman across the street. We might smile warmly, and silently commend the boy for his caring and kindness. This may indeed be his value motivation. On the other hand, the elderly woman may have offered him a reward for his aid so he is acting on self-interest rather than caring. Or, on a more sinister note, the boy may believe his physical proximity will make it easier to snatch her purse and make a run for it once they reach the other, less crowded side of the street.

The knowledge that values-related behavior stems from complex causal factors does not mean that we know what these factors are or how they interact. There is no social scientific multivariate formula that can be used to predict values-related behavior. There is a relationship between moral judgment and behavior, but it is slight. "We accept as essentially accurate the conclusions from the moral judgment-behavior studies that indicate a consistent but low-magnitude correlation" (Rest, 1986, p. 161). For developmental character education, this has a number of implications.

First, the knowledge that values-related behavior is embedded in an intricate context does not exempt such behavior from our moral assessment. Understanding why something occurs must be distinguished from justifying what occurs. In most cases, we may fairly hold persons ethically accountable for their behavior, just as the legal system does when dealing with persons who violate the law.

Relatedly, the fact that values-related behavior often *is* heavily influenced by environmental factors does not mean that it *should* be. Developmental character education advocates expect us to be cognizant of external pressures but also, more important, to think through what behavior would be right in situations that call for a moral decision. We are not exempted from ethical responsibility by pointing to peer pressures or circumstantial pressures that attempt to force our behavior into unacceptable directions.

Developmental character education incorporates the critical ethical distinction between the concepts of *should* and *would*. These must not be confused. It is one thing for students to proclaim what the morally correct thing is to do in a situation—what *should* be done. It is another thing to predict what one is likely to do in a situation—what *would* be done. It must not be assumed that when we have determined the right thing to do, we necessarily will proceed to do the right thing. There is a difference between knowing what right conduct is and actually carrying it out. Developmental character education engages students in considerations of what ethically correct behavior should be and in thinking through how to act on what is ethically correct in spite of psychological or environmental factors mitigating against it.

Some critics of character education emphasize the powerful influence of political, social, and economic factors to the point that attempting to educate for moral responsibility, or virtually anything else, can appear pointless, futile, or even foolhardy. We need to pay attention to these critiques, in part to understand the context in which we work. As educators, however, we work with students and endeavor to provide each of them with the best curriculum and instruction available. That we operate within constraints and our successes are thereby tempered by them is a fact that comes with the territory.

Developmental character education supports the commitment that students should be engaged in the examination of social, political, and economic conditions surrounding actual or proposed behavior. Among other things, this helps students to develop a richer understanding of the context of behavior, to highlight the moral implications of actions in those settings, and to grasp that responsible behavior requires thoughtful effort.

Where does developmental character education stand regarding issues related to the meaning of values? Explicating the meaning of values can appear a rather simple matter but, as was established in earlier chapters, this apparent simplicity is deceptive. Developmental character education recognizes this complexity and takes it seriously in its theory and its curriculum and instruction.

All forms of explicit values education identify a list of values that will provide content for whatever program is being advanced. These lists typically have values that overlap with the lists of other programs and some that are unique to particular programs (Leming, 1996). The general values addressed in developmental character education are the same or similar to those in other character education programs.

The main values addressed in developmental character education are: authority, caring, equality, fairness, honesty, respect, life, loyalty, property, and truth telling. Two initial points need to be made about this list. First, other programs share some or all of these values. Also, this list should not be considered exhaustive. Other value words may be added. What makes developmental character education distinct from other programs is not its list of values but rather how the values are to be treated in the program. Second, the values vary in their degree of generality. The value of respect, for example, can encompass a wide range of types of respect. Similarly, in some situations, caring can encompass courtesy and honesty. The value of life, on the other hand, is more specific in that it addresses situations in which life is taken or threatened.

Listing values, of course, says nothing about whether they are worthwhile. This list, like those of other programs, is likely to be endorsed virtually unanimously by the general population. Such a consensus does not, in itself, make the values worthwhile. A consensus merely means that the vast majority of the public believes something is good. The majority can make moral errors, however. In some nations at some times, genocide or slavery was regarded as morally justified. Those practices are not just, in spite of what the majority might have claimed at those times. Careful thinking and discussion are required in order to determine the rightness or wrongness of moral claims.

From the perspective of developmental character education, the aforementioned values are worthwhile and can be supported by the kind of philosophical thoughtfulness their justification requires. For purposes of this book, I will not elaborate the philosophical arguments establishing their worth. However, in the practice of developmental character education, students regularly are invited to investigate the merits of these values. They are not to be mindlessly endorsed. For example, what authority should be obeyed, and why, in the case of the girl minding the fruit stand? While the values involved in that situation are taken as generally worthwhile, how they should or should not be upheld in specific situations remains an open question. How these values should or should not play out in such situations is a question that developmental character educators raise for critical discussion with their students.

Just as the listing of consensual values does not, in itself, establish their worth, listing them does not presume they have clear definitions. Dictionary-type definitions can be presented, but these often lack the detail needed to make judgments or determine actions in specific situations. For example, we can define honesty as being truthful and genuine, as avoiding fraud and deception. Such a definition is fine as far as it goes. It does not, however, tell us how truthful one must be in order to be honest. Does it require we truthfully tell all of our thoughts and feelings about a topic or just some of them? Is there a limit? If so, where is it and how do we establish it?

Our general definition of honesty does not delimit the range of veracity required in order to be honest. It also does not indicate when we are to be honest. At the extremes, are we to be truthful when directly asked a question by someone, or should we spontaneously express our honest views whenever possible?

Developmental character education provides lists of values and contends that these values are worthwhile as far as they go. Listing presumed worthwhile values has limited utility. These general values provide us with entree into complex moral situations and some common vocabulary for analysis. However, much more thinking and discussion are required before these values come into focus and their situational applicability can be appropriately determined. Developmental character educators understand this and involve their students in such deliberations.

How does developmental character education deal with the problem of conflicts among values? The conception of value issues in developmental character education theory clearly recognizes that conflicts often arise in situations calling for a values-related resolution. Most difficult values-related judgments occur in circumstances when two or more generally worthwhile values come into conflict. That is what makes such judgments difficult.

While developmental character education advocates are fully cognizant of the reality of value conflicts, they also realize that there are differences among persons in their acknowledgment of such conflicts. Adults, adolescents, and children vary in their perception of these conflicts. This is not to say that all adults have the same capacity to see value conflicts, but in general they are more likely to fully detect them than are children.

To elaborate on the previous point, consider the classic vignette known as Sharon's dilemma (Beyer, 1976). The essence of this story is that Sharon and Jill are best friends. They are in a department store and Jill tries on an expensive sweater that she likes. To Sharon's surprise Jill quickly leaves the store with the sweater on under her coat. The store detective sees Jill escaping with the sweater but cannot stop her. He saw the girls together and stops Sharon as she is leaving the store. He asks Sharon to give him the name of the girl who left with the stolen sweater. He says that Sharon will get in trouble if she fails to give her friend's name.

Sharon's dilemma typically is used for discussing the question of whether she should give Jill's name to the detective. Prior to discussion of this question, however, we may ask what values are involved in the story. There are broad developmental differences in how people perceive the values at stake in the story. Young children, for example, may focus only on the value of authority. That is, they are concerned with the illegality of the theft and the power of the store detective (often believed to be equivalent to a police officer). Adolescents may see that the value of authority is involved but also focus on the importance of the value of loyalty to one's friend. Adults typically will see that friendship and authority are involved in the story but also take into account the property rights of the store owner.

There are also developmental differences among people in how troublesome they find the dilemma and in how they resolve it. Adolescents, for example, usually are highly conflicted by the story because of their typical concern with peer and friendship issues. Adults, on the other hand, often focus on the legal and property concerns in the story and find they take precedence over the matter of loyalty to a friend.

Because developmental character education advocates are aware of and sensitive to substantive differences across age groups, they make fewer assumptions about what students know, believe, and can do. The curriculum and instruction of the approach regularly involve students in analysis of value issues and do not presume that they hold common understandings of how values arise in situations or how dilemmas should be resolved.

What is the role of moral principles in developmental character education? Unlike contemporary character education advocates, developmental character education advocates realize that the sound application of moral principles is essential to fully mature moral thought and action. The arguments for this were set out in Chapters 2 and 3. Principles are critical to moral thought and action in a variety of ways. Two are highlighted in the theory of developmental character education.

First, principles help ensure that values are applied in a morally justified way. We have seen that the meaning of values is susceptible to the social context in which they arise. Such values as loyalty, respect, and honesty can be employed for criminal purposes. Terrorists and mobsters are loyal to their bosses, respect them, and are expected to be honest with them if they are to be "good" members of those societies. Sound principles govern the meaning of such values so that they serve worthwhile moral ends. For example, one oft-cited moral principle contends that persons should be treated as ends in themselves, not means to an end. This principle would tell us that loyally obeying an order to kill people in order to advance a political agenda would be wrong. It is using people as means to an end.

A second function of principles is to help us determine what values to uphold in a situation in which values come into conflict. We have seen that equally worthwhile values can come into conflict. This creates a dilemma because we are uncertain which of the conflicting values should take priority in any given ethical predicament. For example, some principles require we take the good of the many over the good of one or a few. One interpretation of this is that just laws should be obeyed and, in most cases, take precedence over personal loyalties. This principle would lead one to conclude, in Sharon's dilemma, that upholding the law against theft morally precludes Jill's desire to protect her friend from the consequences of her law breaking. Similarly, in the previous chapter I provided brief transcripts of two subjects' thinking on the Heinz dilemma. Subject B was able to see that the value of life should take precedence over the other values involved because life was a basic value from which others were derived.

To say that principles are morally important begs the question of which principle or principles should be endorsed. Developmental character education does not dictate any given principle as supreme. Some readers may find this especially frustrating. After all, how can we say that principles are vital and then not say what principles should be promulgated?

One of the reasons developmental character education does not stand on any single moral principle is that moral philosophers, while agreeing on the need for principles, do not agree that any given principle is the crowning one. Debates about principles have gone on as long as recorded philosophy has existed and no doubt will continue.

To say that no single best moral principle has been established that will resolve all ethical dilemmas does not mean that all debate about situational rightness and wrongness is irrelevant and that all moral points of view are equally sound. "Principles" of craven self-interest, clannish loyalty, or slavish obedience to law or some presumed moral authority can violate fundamental human rights and are unsatisfactory as moral standards. Some justifications for our choices are better than others, even if we cannot identify a philosophical consensus on absolute, eternally perfect solutions to all ethical quandaries.

One way in which the practice of developmental character education deals with issues of moral principles is to engage students in deliberations about why they construe particular ethical judgments as better than others. This is done to stimulate the emerging moral reflection of young people. Helping persons recognize ethical values at stake in situations and to think carefully and seriously about them is an exceptional educational achievement. It is one that should not be taken lightly or for granted.

HIGHLIGHTS OF THE THEORY

As we have seen, the theory of developmental character education includes a number of components.

1. Its definition of character education contains some of the components of contemporary character education but supplements and modifies them to embrace developmental concepts.

2. The goal emphasizes the importance of understanding the ethical center of character education. It also underscores the significance of autonomy in mature morality. Truly virtuous behavior is the result of grounded deliberations; it is not mindless conformity to the dictates of some presumed moral authority.
3. Developmental character education theory reflects a well-honed understanding of values. The rationale is conversant with issues related to the justification of values, their definition, and their connection to behavior. It is also aware that value issues occur in a social context that exerts a powerful influence on how persons deal with them.
4. Developmental character education does not shy away from involving students in the complexities of values and value-related behavior. It involves students in considerations of value issues appropriate to their developmental status. It understands that the relationship between values and behavior is both psychologically and philosophically problematic and does not decree simple answers when there are legitimately complex questions.

WHY WE NEED DEVELOPMENTAL CHARACTER EDUCATION

Now that the sources and major configurations of developmental character education have been established, it is appropriate to note why its advocates believe it should be a substantial part of the school curriculum. Many programs vie for limited space in the curriculum, and strong arguments must be made for those that prevail.

I believe there is growing awareness that schooling must begin to take seriously its typically titular role of preparing young people to be productive and responsible members of society. This always has been a generally stated purpose of schooling, especially public schooling, but rarely has been treated with the same level of commitment accorded to academic subjects. This is especially true in secondary schools.

What would it mean for schooling to engage in pursuing the goal of a productive and responsible citizenry? There are, of course, numerous proposed answers to this question. Regardless of how one addresses the question, however, there is no doubt that some form of curricular treatment of values necessarily will be part of the response. Althof and Berkowitz (2006) offer a careful argument showing that character education needs to be a critical element in any conception of citizenship education.

Given that some treatment of value issues must be part of the citizenship mission of schooling, what treatment is best thought through and worthy of support? For a number of reasons I believe developmental character education is the strongest candidate for this endorsement.

Developmental character education is designed explicitly to influence how students interact with one another, with groups, and with society. Its focus is on promoting responsible, thoughtful, well-grounded ethical thinking and behavior.

Developmental character education engages students in deep reflection about the meaning of values and their appropriate connection to behavior. This work is consistent with the intellectual purposes of education and is particularly integral to the study of literature and social studies. Developmental character education does not involve indoctrinating students into some simple set of presumed right answers to perplexing questions.

Developmental character education is distinctive in understanding that the way in which value issues should be addressed will vary depending on the maturational status of students. What is appropriate for young children will not be useful with older children, and vice versa. To be effective, curriculum and instruction in character education must be attuned to developmental differences in students, just as we take into account differential reading abilities of students.

Developmental character education argues that the need for sound treatment of values in schooling is not an educational fad. Some proponents of contemporary character education emphasize that their curriculum is necessary for responding to high rates of destructive behavior among young people. Presumably, if such behavior diminished, there would be a diminished need for character education. Developmental character education believes that educating a citizenry to be thoughtful about value issues is a perennial necessity for a healthy and just society. Developmental character education is not a response to current high rates of destructive behavior.

Chapter 6

The Practice of Developmental Character Education

In previous chapters I have described the character education terrain and argued that developmental character education should have a prominent position in the landscape. Much of this argument has been analytic, psychological, theoretical, and philosophical. I have described developmental character education and how its conceptualization and rationale overcome certain deficiencies of contemporary character education. I also have claimed that developmental character education provides the soundest basis for shaping values education curricula for our youth. Here I will provide more detail about the practice of developmental character education, offering guidelines and suggestions for teachers to employ when selecting curriculum and instruction suitable for their students, when modifying current instructional materials and practices, or when creating curricula anew.

The remainder of this chapter presents ideas, drawn from a developmental perspective, for both the content and methods of developmental character education. The suggestions presented are best understood as orienting recommendations. My hope is that they provide concepts and direction for the thinking of teachers and curriculum developers hoping to make character education a well-justified and effective educational program.

DEVELOPMENTAL CURRICULUM CONTENT

Teachers engaged in character education must decide what materials to employ with their students. All teachers make age-related judgments about reading level, conceptual difficulty, and other matters when selecting and creating their curricula. Age-related considerations are, of course, pertinent. As will be presented shortly, from a developmental perspective, additional questions are germane. It must be noted that answers to these questions reflect informed professional judgments, as do most educational decisions, and are not products of hard, experimental science. It also should be noted that the broad developmental schemes presented earlier do not offer precise characterizations of individual students. Instead they give us concepts providing a rough boundary for what is relevant to include in the curriculum at different levels of schooling.

The central content question here is: Are the value issues in the curriculum developmentally appropriate?

The value topics in a current or proposed character education curriculum need to be assessed to determine their fit with the dominant developmental status of the students. As was explained in Chapter 4, these developmental concerns are not explicitly vocalized by students but are identified as common to particular phases of development. The curricular judgments to be made are whether the value issues are likely to be engaging to students and developmentally relevant, or whether they are too remote from students' experience or needs. This does not mean selecting issues that students necessarily will enjoy or revel in exploring. There are some issues we want students to address whether they find them engaging or not, such as how children should relate to one another during informal, unstructured school time.

Elementary School

For *elementary-age* students, a variety of value issues and topics are especially relevant:

1. The curriculum should involve students in defining values. These students have heard value admonitions, such as do what you are told, be nice to one another, tell the truth, work hard, and the like. Typically, however, they have not had classroom time spent in putting value labels on these exhortations. In effect, we want the curriculum to begin teaching students the vocabulary of values.

Teaching the vocabulary of values is part of the goal of helping persons perceive situations in which values are at stake. In an evaluation study of a character education curriculum, Leming (2000) found that young children can effectively learn a vocabulary of values. Children in the experimental groups received 14 lessons focusing on seven values from the Heartwood character education curriculum (Heartwood Institute, 1992). The experimental group could define such values as honesty and respect and use them correctly in sentences much more accurately than the control groups.

2. The curriculum should involve students in identifying value issues in both fictional and real situations. Simple identifications would involve

students reading or being told of someone acting on the basis of a value. For example, a babysitter asks a child whether he would like candy before going to bed. The child tells the babysitter that his mother does not let him have candy before going to bed. In this case, students should be able to identify the child's statement as an example of honesty. Counter examples can be used as well. For example, the child asks for candy before bed and says that his mother always gives him some, although she does not. Here, lying would be an example of someone being dishonest.

3. In addition to defining and identifying values, students should be asked to explain, in their own words, why the value is worthwhile. With honesty, for example, the curriculum should ask them, after they have mastered its definition and are relatively facile in identifying instances of it, why honesty is a good thing. This is part of the general character education task of encouraging student commitment to central moral values.

Setting out reasons for why honesty is a good value is developmentally appropriate. From the moral development point of view children can begin to see that reasoning is an important part of decision making. Also, understanding honesty is clearly relevant to Eriksonian issues of trust versus mistrust, which are significant to young children. Knowing that they are being treated with honesty by an adult helps develop a sense of trust between children and adults.

4. It is common for character education curricula for the elementary grades to feature children's literature. Often such literature is employed as a means of showing children upstanding values behavior on the part of real or fictional characters (Bennett, 1996).

Good-quality literature also creates numerous occasions for children to consider value issues. Literature provides opportunities to identify examples of values and also to begin discovering and discussing moral issues.

Characters in fairy tales and other forms of children's literature frequently encounter situations in which they make value decisions. They may, for example, disobey an authority, mislead or lie to another character, take another's property, and so on. Using these stories, the curriculum should ask children to talk about whether the character made the right decision and why the decision was right or wrong.

Cognitive moral developmentalists have shown that younger children take into account issues related to punishment, authority, self-interest, and to some extent the views of their peers when making ethical judgments. Stories presenting moral questions for discussion by children should include information on how those issues, or some of them, are involved. This provides children with content for their deliberations. For example, if the story about lying to the babysitter is used, it should include information about what punishment the mother would employ if the child took candy before bedtime, why the mother had the candy policy, and, perhaps, how much the child liked the particular candy involved.

5. Also appropriate for elementary school, but certainly not limited to that level, is providing students opportunities to consider how values have been employed in their own behavior and that of others. When discussing courtesy, for example, children can be asked to report instances of people acting respectfully toward others or times at which they have acted respectfully. They also can report instances in which disrespectful behavior occurred. The curriculum should help students think about the values-related behavior of others but also of themselves.

Another exercise that can be useful here is to have children, alone or in groups, create an ideal school where everyone treated one another properly. They would explain what went on in this school and their classroom on a typical day, including recess and lunchtime. Each student or group would explain why its creation was ideal and what values students and adults exhibited. Then students would look at their existing school and classroom and describe how, if at all, they met the features of their ideal school and classroom. To the extent improvements were needed in the behavior of people in their real school and classroom, they would explain how that might be accomplished. They might propose some policies that could be taken to the teacher or principal for consideration.

6. The stories employed in the curriculum also should contain enough detail about the attributes and values of the characters to facilitate identifying their points of view about what occurs in the story. Part of the ongoing practice of developmental character education asks students to recognize the perspective of all persons involved in a situation. There must be enough information for young students to intelligently carry this out.

Developmentally, young children are typically very concrete thinkers. That is why the feelings and thoughts of people in the stories being discussed should be spelled out quite clearly. Children's ability to imagine the points of view of others is much more limited than that of adolescents and adults.

To summarize, the value issues and topics to be introduced to young children include: (1) naming and defining values; (2) identifying values in real or imaginary circumstances; (3) developing explanations for why certain values are worthwhile; (4) considering the rightness or wrongness of value-related behaviors; (5) reflecting on how values operate in one's own life; and, (6) identifying or describing the perspectives of others.

Middle and High School

For *early to late adolescents,* additional values issue and topics become salient.

1. The curriculum should provide opportunities for students to make the philosophical distinction between moral and nonmoral value issues. Generally, moral value issues affect the rights and well-being of others. Such values as life and liberty fit this category. Nonmoral value issues are our views of good and bad applied to matters that do not affect the fundamental rights of others. For example, our preferences for foods, entertainment, arts, and so on, reflect value judgments but they are nonmoral.

The distinction between moral and nonmoral value issues is consequential. As a general rule, we want moral decisions to be made with thoughtfulness and care. They are weighty matters deserving our best considered judgments. We generally judge nonmoral value issues as having less or no impact on fundamental human rights and not requiring such serious deliberation as do moral value issues. Someone's preference for television situation comedies over another's preference for dramas may stir vigorous discussion, but is of less significance than one's decision on capital punishment. Steven Pinker (2008) puts it this way:

> Prohibitions of rape and murder, for example, are felt not to be matters of local custom but to be universally and objectively warranted. One can easily say, "I don't like brussels sprouts, but I don't care if you eat them," but no one would say, "I don't like killing, but I don't care if you murder someone." (p. 34)

The moral/nonmoral distinction is not firmly etched. There are times when the line is blurred and requires analysis. In normal human discourse the distinction is rarely made. It is common for adolescents, and adults for that matter, to debate with passion and emotionality nonmoral value preferences for music, movies, fashions, and the like. The intensity of these opinions can equal that related to moral value issues such as proposed policies that would limit freedom of speech or privacy rights.

While equal passion may be expended on nonmoral and moral value issues, developmental character education curriculum should help students make the distinction. Also, the curriculum should engage students primarily in moral value issues, not nonmoral. Obviously, there is serious human importance in how we as citizens make decisions about moral value issues. Students should know when they are confronting such issues and give them the deep attention they deserve. Moral debate is often passionate, but passionate discourse is not, in itself, moral deliberation.

Before presenting a value issue for debate, the curriculum should provide opportunities for students to analyze the issue. Attention should be directed to activities such as defining the central values at stake in a situation and identifying the human consequences of different decisions prior to discussion of the rightness or wrongness of decisions under consideration. In the Heinz dilemma, for example, students should be able to identify that the druggist's property rights are involved as well as the law against stealing and also Heinz's wife's right to life.

2. The curriculum should involve students in identifying value issues in a variety of settings. These may include international, national, state, local, and school issues. There are numerous ways this can be done, but the curriculum should have students actively engaged in identifying issues that reflect the social, economic, and political realities of their lives. Students should discuss the issues with teacher facilitation, and teachers should avoid, as much as is reasonably possible, telling the students what value issues are involved. As students become older and more independent, they need to know, without a teacher pointing them out, when they are encountering value issues and what is at stake in their resolution.

In addition to identifying value issues in a variety of settings, the curriculum also should ensure that students recognize a wide range of value issues. It is relatively easy to find questions related to freedom of speech or human life, but other value issues should be recognized as well. Situations involving such values as equality, honesty, loyalty, property rights, respect, and authority also should be part of the curriculum. For example, someone who owns a large tract of land in a community may plan to develop a project with many houses. Opponents may object that this is a threat to the environment and the quality of life in the community. Analytically, this is a situation in which such values as property rights, respect, and authority are involved. The teacher may wish to modify the original issue to see whether students' initial views change, such as specifying that the development is for low-income families.

3. The cognitive developmental level of most adolescents permits them to understand that multiple values may be involved in a particular situation. It is developmentally appropriate for such students to be involved in analyzing and

discussing increasingly complex dilemmas in which values come into conflict. The curriculum should provide ample opportunities for such deliberations.

A key time for identifying and discussing moral principles is when students are wrestling with situations in which values conflict. The curriculum should use these occasions as times to consider principles. Students should be asked to identify what general ideas (principles) lie behind the resolutions they find best justified and those they find least defensible.

In addition to fictional dilemmas, the curriculum should have students ponder real-life dilemmas. These may be situations that students have identified, as in point 2 above, or the teacher has selected and that are consistent with the academic course of study. For example, history teachers might choose dilemmas germane to immigration when that topic is being addressed (Lockwood & Harris, 1985). English teachers, of course, have at their disposal multiple value issues that arise in literature, both fiction and nonfiction.

4. The curriculum should provide situations in which students can engage in taking the perspectives of a wide variety of persons and roles. The central questions of how another person perceives a situation, thinks about it, and feels about it, and how the consequences of a decision would affect the person, can be expanded vastly compared with what is appropriate for young children.

Adolescents are notoriously concerned with peer relations, and imagining the views of their peer group is relatively easy. Perspective taking, however, needs to be extended to others and should include parents, siblings, adolescents not in their peer group, teachers, other adults in the community, and persons of different ethnic backgrounds and economic status. Taking the perspective of others not known to students also should be required. The perspectives of members of groups other than one's own and groups more geographically remote need to be considered as well. For example, students might question why so many people in the Middle East seem to hate America. Activities can be designed for students to try to understand the perspectives of these others. Of course, understanding why this hatred exists is different from justifying it.

The curriculum must provide not only opportunities for perspective taking, but also the information necessary to make such hypothesizing realistic. Relevant information about others needs to be available so that students do not simply assume that everyone else is like them and would have the same perceptions and feelings about events.

5. The curriculum must make it clear that there is a critical distinction between understanding the perspectives of others and approving those per-

spectives. From the standpoint of developmental character education, sound moral judgments take other human beings seriously. To do this, one needs to discern the views of others and how they may be affected by the consequences of different decisions.

While a mature moral agent considers the views of others, he or she may not endorse those views as ethically relevant or defensible. They may or may not be. A commonly made error is to confuse understanding with justification. There are some who believe that rich understandings of other persons or cultures is the equivalent of finding them morally defensible. They may or may not be. As an extreme example, one might study why infanticide is practiced in some cultures. Understanding the action is different from determining whether it is morally justified. Making ethical judgments of others is a different enterprise from seeking information that aids in understanding others.

6. When value issues are being pondered, the curriculum must provide activities in which students think about their own past or future value-related behavior. Moral deliberation, considering the rightness or wrongness of one's past or potential behavior, is a central aspect of developmental character education.

The curriculum engages students in much "should talk" related to value issues, that is, discussions of whether others should have done what they did, or what they should do in a current or future circumstance. The curriculum also should engage students in much "would talk," that is, thoughtful consideration about what one has done or would do in particular situations. Students could, for example, imagine themselves in Sharon's position, wrestling with whether she should report the name of her friend who stole the sweater from the department store. They can discuss what they think they would do and what they think they should do.

What is pivotal here is that students connect their own shoulds and woulds in such a way that they contemplate not only the psychological question of what they are likely to do but also the moral question of what should be done. The ideal outcome is that their shoulds inform their woulds. The goal is for students to understand, be committed to, and do the right thing.

7. The developmentally appropriate contexts in which the curriculum raises value questions for adolescents should include issues associated with peer groups. These would include obligations related to friendship, dealing with peer pressures, stresses associated with affiliation, and so on. These are especially relevant for both early and later adolescent students.

Older adolescents may deal with value issues that arise in job-related settings, their own and those of others, and in future career choices and aspirations. Content also should be related to citizenship value issues and other matters that arise as a consequence of being members of their particular communities.

8. Character education curricular content for adolescents confronts institutional constraints more limiting than those in typical elementary settings. At least two deserve note. First, secondary teachers, particularly at the high school level, are not inclined to see themselves as character educators. They are trained, licensed, hired, and personally inclined to focus on instruction in their academic specialties. These teachers, understandably, concentrate their efforts on teaching their subjects. Second, school days are organized for coursework in subject areas. Little time is allocated for nonacademic pursuits, even if they are believed worthwhile.

These constraints are exacerbated by the emphasis on academic standards and testing, often with school funding dependent on test results. Teachers and other school personnel increasingly are pressured to stress academic content likely to be tested and to teach students how to take tests. Current federal law intensifies this emphasis by officially evaluating schools on the basis of their students' test scores. Whether it should or should not be, the content of students' character is not tested as part of this evaluation of schooling.

These constraints can be daunting to the character education advocate, but they are not insurmountable. For one thing, academic achievement and the promotion of sound character are complementary aims of schooling and together enhance the quality of students' education. This complementarity has been documented recently and in the past (Berman, 2004; Wynne & Walberg, 1985/1986). There are also secondary schools that are successful in organizing for effectiveness in both character and academic education (Berman, 1997; Lickona & Davidson, 2005).

One educationally sound practice is to connect character content with that of the academic disciplines. This is not some misplaced, procrustean enterprise. Most school subjects have value issues embedded in them, and their analysis and discussion enrich student understanding of the disciplines as well as contributing to good character development. There are a number of illustrations of how this is being done (Ryan, 1993; Simon, 2001).

To summarize, the value issues and topics that should be part of the developmental character education curriculum for adolescents include: (1) understanding and working with the moral/nonmoral distinction; (2) identifying a wide range of value issues in a wide range of settings; (3) recognizing situations in which values conflict and debating how these conflicts should be resolved and what principles govern these proposed resolutions; (4) engaging in perspective taking of a broad range of persons and evaluating those perspectives; (5) introspection about one's views of rightness and wrongness as they apply to the behavior of others and oneself; (6) values-related issues that arise in peer relations and current and potential future employment and citizenship settings; and (7) value issues that arise within academic subject matter.

DEVELOPMENTAL INSTRUCTIONAL PRACTICES

Value topics that should be relevant and engaging to students at different developmental levels were spelled out in the previous section. In this section I will present ideas for shaping teaching methods to be appropriate and effective for students at these different levels. As with the value topics, this listing is in no way exhaustive or detailed in its specifications. The intent is to make suggestions that encourage the instructor to modify current teaching methods or to tackle new ones. Experienced, skilled teachers enjoy evaluating and applying different ideas; they do not require a step-by-step recipe book and frequently resent being told to employ one.

The methods presented here are all intended to actively immerse students in learning. Didactic methods such as lecturing are not discussed. This is not to preclude the use of didactic methods in developmental character education. They can be useful in presenting students with information relevant to a character-related topic. Methods promoting active learning dominate in developmental character education because, in the final analysis, students will be making their own decisions on critical value questions. They will be assessing situations, considering and evaluating behavioral options, and choosing how to behave. Students will not, nor should they, have some moral authority looking over their shoulders dictating to them the right thing to do.

The following activities are organized by method. Unlike the earlier claims that some developmental character education topics are more appropriate for younger children than adolescents, similar methods are suggested for all developmental levels. For example, it is appropriate to use discussion methods with all students. Developmental perspectives provide guidance on how these methods can be shaped to be most effective with students at different levels.

Role Playing

This method has students assume the persona of real or fictional characters. As these characters, they act as they presumably would in some real or imaginary situation. As will be shown, role playing can serve a variety of character education purposes.

The role playing may be somewhat scripted (students have set things they are to say and do as the story they are enacting unfolds) or more or less improvised (students are told something of their character's beliefs, personality, etc., and then act as they believe the character would in those circumstances). I say more or less because, for example, the script could be highly detailed or loosely outlined. Similarly, a great deal of information or only a few traits about the character to be portrayed could be provided.

For *elementary-age* students, the role-playing performances should be of relatively short duration. This is in part because these performances occur in front of classmates whose attention spans can be fleeting. As a general rule, depending on the instructional objective, these role plays should be more scripted than less and, if improvised, more controlled than free.

For these children, role playing can serve a number of developmental character education aims. For example, students may have spent time defining some basic values such as honesty, respect, property rights, fairness, and so forth. A group of students can be selected to act out a scene involving one of these values. One student may be asked to demonstrate acting on the basis of the value or failing to act on its basis. Classmates observing the performance have to identify what value is being portrayed and how it is being portrayed. Observers also can discuss other ways the value could be acted upon or, if there was failure to act, what the character could have done to demonstrate positive action on the value. This use of role playing addresses the goal of helping students identify values and consider what they look like in behavior.

Another form of role playing for elementary-age children is to complete an imaginary end to a story involving a value decision. The class reads or hears a story in which a character or characters confront a situation in which they must make a decision involving a value—to tell or not tell the truth, for example. A group of students may be chosen to portray the characters and to act out a variety of alternative decisions that might be made and the consequences that occurred subsequently. Observers can discuss what values the characters chose to act upon and whether the consequences were likely or there were others that could occur. This invites students to think about how values are involved in decisions and what possible effects they may engender.

One purpose of developmental character education is for students to improve their abilities to understand the perspectives of others. Role playing can be used for this purpose. Students can be selected to act out a story, not highly scripted, in which each of them plays a different person in a different position. For example, one might be a new student, a teacher, a police officer, a parent, and so on. After the scenario has been played out, the actors can talk about what it was like to see the situation from the perspective of another person. Observers also can discuss their perceptions of the likely perspectives held by the characters.

For *early to late adolescents,* role playing also can be an effective way to pursue developmental character education goals. These students typically can sustain their plays for longer periods than can elementary-age students. Properly organized improvised role plays are also more productive with these older students because they have more experiences to draw on when developing their characters. Effective role playing requires that teachers have developed a trusting relationship in the classroom so that students do not ridicule the "performances" of others.

Role plays that portray circumstances in which values come into conflict are effective with adolescents. Stories in which a character or characters are confronted with moral dilemmas involving multiple values can be acted out. For example, students could role play the characters in Sharon's dilemma, which I described earlier. In these stories the characters may make decisions or the story may stop at the point at which a decision is called for. In both cases, observers can discuss the decision(s) made, what values held sway, and whether the decisions were appropriate or inappropriate. If the story stops at the decision point, observers can discuss what decision(s) they believe would be best and why.

Role-playing scenarios may be provided by the teacher and derived from academic subjects. History students might portray advisors to President Truman when he was confronted with the decision whether to employ the atomic bomb in Japan. Literature students can act out the parts of Richard Wright (1996) and the adults and adolescents around him when he makes a decision whether or not to participate in a cheating scheme. It is also pertinent to have scenarios involving contemporary circumstances at a job site, settings in the business world, post-secondary education, or the military.

While role-playing scenarios may be set by the teacher, students also can create them. Small groups of students can be assigned the task of writing a short scenario in which characters confront a value dilemma. They may be asked to create a story that depicts a "typical" adolescent problem with peers, adults, or persons in positions of authority. These students then may act out the story or have another group act it out.

The cognitive development of most adolescents permits them to contemplate a variety of factors in a given situation. This makes it possible for role-taking activities to consider multiple perspectives. Role playing can serve this function. In role-playing scenarios with many actors, observers can be asked to describe and assess the differing perspectives of the actors. Also, students who have played the roles should be asked to describe their thoughts and feelings as they observed the situation from the standpoint of the person they were acting out.

It is often both interesting and useful to have the same scenario played out by different groups of students. For example, two or three groups may be formed to play out the same situation. The groups are separated as they plan their performances so that they do not know in advance how their peers acted out the situation. After the exhibitions, students discuss the similarities and differences in how they portrayed the problem.

Writing Assignments

Students at all age levels are given writing tasks for a variety of educational purposes. These assignments also can contribute to character education. Writing assignments can be employed as follow-up reflections to many character education activities as well as be character education activities in themselves.

Some *elementary-age* students in the very earliest grades are unlikely to write much beyond a few sentences and might better be asked to draw a response to an assignment rather than write one. Teachers are in the best situation to determine the extent to which writing assignments should be made. Older students, of course, become capable of writing coherent sentences and paragraphs.

The students may be asked to draw or write the meaning of specific values. The students then will show and tell what they created to explain the meaning of the value. For instance, they may be asked to create examples of honesty. Students then can discuss the differences and similarities in their portrayals of the value.

Students can be asked to keep journals for a specific period of time. For example, they may be asked to record instances in which they saw or encountered values being enacted or violated. They should describe the behavior that reflected the value or should have reflected it. They also should describe how they reacted to the situation. The teacher can discuss the journals with individual students or have students present them to the group for discussion.

If discussed publicly, the names of persons in the situation should be changed or other effective ways of protecting their identities should be enforced. Younger students in particular are inclined to follow the teacher's authority and rarely object to sharing their journals or other information. When journals or other experiences potentially may be made public, teachers must take the initiative to control what is presented. Classrooms must not become settings in which the privacy rights of students or others are threatened or violated.

Students may be asked to write about a story they have read or have had read to them. They might write their opinion about a values-based action taken by a character or, if the story is stopped at a decision-making point, write what decision they think should be made. Older students can share their writing assignment and, in pairs, identify the similarities and differences in what they wrote. Pairs then can report to the whole class, and the teacher can record the similarities and differences on the board. A group discussion about these may follow. Among other things, the group can speculate on why there were similarities and differences.

The aforementioned assignment also can be modified for perspective-taking purposes. Students are asked to describe the thoughts and feelings of different characters in a story as they confront a common situation.

Writing assignments are also effective means of helping students ponder their own behavior. They are asked to describe situations in which they did or did not act upon the basis of some specified value. To the extent possible, they should describe why they behaved the way they did, how they felt about it, how it affected others, and whether they would do it again. As a general rule, this type of assignment should be seen only by the teacher or used for dialogue between the teacher and individual student. Understandably, students are often reluctant to reveal and discuss this type of information in front of their peers. As mentioned above, the privacy rights of involved parties must be protected in activities such as this.

Writing assignments for *early to late adolescents* also can effectively serve developmental character education ends. Students can examine a value-rich current issue, either school-related, local, national, or international. They then, alone or with another, write an editorial expressing their views on the value-laden problem. The editorials can be compared and contrasted with those of classmates. The class may choose to send one or more to a local newspaper or the school newspaper.

The journal assignments mentioned for elementary school students can be adapted easily for high school students. The journal can be used for recording instances in which students encountered values-related situations. It is also constructive for students to record instances in which they had to make a values-based decision. The decision should be reported, the value(s) involved explicated, and the thinking that went into the decision explained. Students also should be asked to evaluate their decision. Was it right? Did they have other options? Would they do it again?

Creative-writing assignments offer a plethora of character education possibilities. Students can write a play or movie script in which characters confront a values-related issue and deal with it in some manner suitable for dramatic or comedic enacting. The play then can be acted out or the movie videotaped. Observers then are assigned to write a review of the performance, with a focus on how realistic the value issue was and their evaluation of how it was resolved in the performance.

Another creative-writing project that is especially effective with early adolescents is story writing for children. The students are assigned, alone or in pairs or groups, to write a story that tries to teach younger children some important value lesson, such as how and why to be honest or respectful. Students also can provide illustrations for their stories. The books then can be given to teachers in the elementary schools in the district for their comments or use. If students are involved in cross-age teaching projects, the books can be used as materials for reading lessons and discussions.

Writing also can be done in response to lessons in which students carry out a mock trial. The trials may be based on value-rich fictional cases or actual historical or contemporary controversial events. Students working as defense or prosecution teams have to prepare their cases arguing why their value position should prevail. Students on the jury then must make their decision. Prior to that decision, however, each juror should write his or her opinion on the case. Writing one's thinking prior to any discussion is generally an appropriate activity. It helps ensure that students do some independent thinking and do not simply agree with whatever a dominant peer says.

The Internet also can be employed for character-related writing assignments. Increasingly, classes in some schools are connected by the Internet to peers in other parts of the country or the world. Whole-class discussions of values-related issues can be orchestrated by the respective classroom teachers. Also, students who are Internet penpals with peers in another school can discuss, one-on-one, value issues that they see as pertinent to themselves. These writing assignments serve to keep value issues focal points for adolescent contemplations.

Discussion

Discussion is the centerpiece classroom activity for developmental character education. Classroom discussion is the vehicle that permits students to hear ideas, express ideas, test ideas, and elaborate their emerging social and philosophical theories of values and how they should operate to guide human behavior. Unfortunately, in my experience, leading effective discussions requires a degree of proficiency that often is underemphasized in teacher education programs.

Because this is not a methods textbook, I will not provide detailed recommendations on how best to conduct discussions. I will, however, offer some general comments on effective discussion leading for any grade level.

1. Be clear on the purpose of the discussion. A variety of educational aims may be pursued through discussion. For any given discussion-based lesson, the objectives need to be clear to both the teacher and the students. At a minimum, this provides criteria for determining what counts as relevant contributions to the discussion. For example, if the purpose is to hypothesize on the perspectives of different parties in a value-related situation, comments about one's own opinion on how the situation should be resolved are not relevant.

2. Do not assume that students know how to carry out productive discussions. In addition to having a clear purpose for the discussion, the teacher should have a clear idea of the features of a good discussion. Such features include staying on the topic, listening to one another, not interrupting, and so on. These need to be communicated clearly to students. Most students, young children as well as older adolescents, do not automatically engage in effective discussions. They must be taught how to do so. Using videotapes for evaluation of the strengths and weaknesses of the discussion is helpful. Teachers who take the time to teach how to have a discussion are rewarded with the quality of future discussions held by their students.

3. Record the major points made during the discussion. This can be done on an overhead projector or the chalkboard. These should be written in the students' words, not as elegant teacher paraphrases. Keeping a record of the points made in the discussion helps make it clear that the discourse is important. Using the students' own wording conveys that their views are worthwhile and being taken seriously.

4. When debating a moral dilemma, be certain to distinguish between "shoulds" and "woulds." Discussions of shoulds deal with students' judgments about the rightness or wrongness of a decision made or contemplated. Discussions of woulds deals with students' deliberations on what they or others would do in the situation. These are both topics that can be worthy of discussion, but they should not be mixed together because they require different forms of thought and clarifying one is not the equivalent of clarifying the other.

5. Vary discussion formats. Whole-class discussions are often productive but invariably some students will be reluctant to participate. Having students discuss the central question in small groups prior to a whole-class discussion can be helpful. Each student in the group can be assigned a role (facilitator, note taker, etc.) to ensure an orderly discussion. The groups should be given a clear task for their time together. For example, they may be required to identify two arguments in favor and two against a central question.

Another format often is called a "fish bowl" discussion. About half the class is placed in a circle in the center of the room. They discuss the central question while observers are given an assignment to complete as they watch the discussion. For example, they may be asked to identify the strongest and weakest argument they heard and to state why they made those judgments.

A variation on the fish bowl discussion is one in which the observers act as consultants. Each discussant is paired with an observer/consultant. The consultant's job is to think of things the partner might add to the discussion to strengthen the case or to challenge other discussants. The teacher may stop the discussion periodically to permit time for the consultants to talk with their partners.

Teachers can generate a variety of formats for discussion. There are also published works that are helpful in planning discussions (Henning, 2008; Parker, 2003; Simon, 2001).

6. Provide a conclusion to the discussion. Discussions should not simply die of their own accord or end by the ringing of the passing bell. The teacher should provide time at the end for an educational summary. For most discussion topics, there should not be an effort to force consensus in the group. The teacher may outline the major points made during the discussion or ask students to do so. Students may be asked to describe something they learned from the discussion. Students also may be asked to identify an argument or point that came up in the discussion that they had not heard or thought about before. The summary activity helps students recognize that discussions are not simply the airing of views but have the deeper educational meaning of promoting thoughtful reflection.

Teachers are often uncertain whether, or in what circumstances, they should disclose their own views on the topic under discussion. There is no established answer to this question. However the teacher decides to deal with this issue, he or she must be certain not to foreclose students' opportunities to discuss the topic. If the teacher chooses to disclose, he or she must be clear about the reasons for doing so. There are a number of roles the teacher can play in discussions, such as moderator, advocate, or judge. Lockwood (1996) has outlined some of these roles and explained the rationale for enacting them.

7. There are also numerous out-of-classroom activities that can be valuable for character education purposes. Community service projects, experiential learning projects, and field trips can focus on values-related issues. For example, children visiting a home for the elderly can prepare interviews in which they explore the value opinions of the residents. Projects in the community can be devised with the intent of exploring an ethic of caring for others.

Cross-age teaching or tutoring is also an effective out-of-classroom learning activity for character education. If, for example, older students are helping younger students read, they also should engage the younger students in discussion of the values involved in the stories and what they mean.

In all cases, out-of-classroom activities should be followed up by serious reflection by the students. This can be done by keeping journals, discussion, or both. Students should be asked to summarize what they learned from these exercises and how values played out in their activities. These reflections help clarify and solidify what students have learned from their experiences.

SUMMARY

This chapter was intended to provide some examples of how developmental character education can play out in practice. It showed how character- and values-related topics can be coordinated with students' probable developmental status at the elementary and secondary levels, and provided suggestions for modifying teaching methods to make them developmentally appropriate.

These illustrations of developmental character education practices are neither exhaustive nor exclusive to the approach. The hope is that teachers and curriculum developers will use the framework to generate their own ideas for effectively implementing this conception of character education. There is no "official" developmental character education curriculum. Many, but certainly not all, of the curricular suggestions of contemporary character education advocates can be altered to become consistent with the developmental perspective (Lickona, 1991, 2004; Ryan & Bohlin, 1999).

As I have noted, there is a staggering array of materials and methods available commercially, some of which can be shaped for developmental purposes. Because of this profusion, I have avoided citing any of them lest I leave some out or appear to be endorsing some. Berkowitz and Bier (2005) examined and evaluated a number of available approaches to character education. The reader should find their report valuable.

Finally, this outline of developmental character education curriculum and instruction flows from the assumption that most school-based character education occurs in classrooms. There are highly promising character education schools but they are clearly the exception (Lickona & Davidson, 2005). Consequently, this chapter has focused on what can be accomplished in the classroom.

Epilogue

As the most widely recognized term for contemporary values education, character education deserves careful attention. At a minimum, we need to know what it is and why it is presumed to be valuable. These two issues were discussed in previous chapters. In this summary epilogue I will comment on them briefly.

WHAT IS CHARACTER EDUCATION?

The phrase *character education* has dominated professional discourse about values and schooling for at least a decade. Educators are accustomed to hearing it. Government officials and the general public are growing acquainted with the term. Although character education has become a common topic in discussions of schooling and educational policy, its definition requires a sharper focus. When we use a term frequently, its familiarity can lead us to believe we agree on what it means—even when we do not. Such is the case with character education.

The commonality of the term belies the absence of definitional consensus. At character education conferences, for example, scores of sessions are devoted to presentations on character education and its practice. Anyone who attends such sessions must come away wondering how all these varied practices can be considered part of the same conception of values education.

Further evidence of character education's definitional ambiguity can be found when one reads surveys of school districts' character education practices. An extraordinary variety of instructional programs are reported as examples of character education in these schools, but they lack clear, concise, uniform definitions.

There are a number of reasons why a generally agreed-upon definition of character education is needed. For one, school leaders interested in exploring whether character education should be part of their curriculum need to know what it is that is being touted. This will permit them to examine available curriculum materials, as well as to identify relevant research on their effectiveness. Political leaders interested in promoting legislation about and funding for character education need to be clear about what they are addressing. A definition is also necessary for researchers and program evaluators. Researchers attempting to ascertain the effects of character education need to know precisely what it is they are to assess.

In Chapter 1 a working definition of contemporary character education was presented, after a careful review of the published works of major character education advocates and examples of the practices they endorse. By ascertaining the common conceptions of theory and practice in these writings, set forth the following definition:

> Character education is any school-initiated program designed to shape directly and systematically the behavior of young people by teaching explicitly the nonrelativistic values believed to directly bring about good behavior.

This definition has been useful in assessing the strengths and weaknesses of current character education theory and practice. This study has led to the redefinition and reconfiguration of a conception of character education that preserves the strengths of current approaches and provides substantive improvements to theory and practice. For reasons that should be clear by now, this reconfiguration I call developmental character education. It should be noted that character education occurs in nonschool settings as well. For purposes of this book, however, the focus is on school-based character education.

THE VALUE OF DEVELOPMENTAL CHARACTER EDUCATION

Schools have always, in one form or another, engaged in values education either implicitly or explicitly. At a minimum, we expect schools to prepare students with knowledge and skills related to academic subject matter. We also expect schools to contribute to the well-being of society by preparing students to become adults who contribute to the quality of society—citizens who have not only academic knowledge and skills, but also the capacity and disposition to treat others with dignity and respect. Often called citizenship education, direct efforts to influence the values of young people in the service of a better society are now referred to commonly as character education.

The promotion of good character is something that schools can do in ways distinct from other social institutions such as families and religions. Families and religions, of course, have strong influences on the character of youth. The structure of schooling, however, can contribute uniquely to character development.

One of the particular features of schools that makes a singular contribution to character education possible is the diversity of their populations. This diversity can include such things as ethnicity, socioeconomic status, race, physical and intellectual challenges, gender, interests, and religion. This diversity provides the potential for students to hear, consider, and discuss a variety of values-related issues from a wide range of different perspectives. It also, to some extent, provides a social setting in which students can act on the basis of emerging value orientations and, ideally, be called upon to reflect on the values and behavior of themselves and others. Character education that helps students intelligently confront and engage in values-based discussion in a diverse setting can offer a realistic and sound preparation for the challenges and responsibilities of living in a democratic society.

One of the more powerful qualities of the rationale for character education is its recognition that good citizenship involves much more than the relationship of persons to their governments. Character education is concerned with all aspects of values-related citizen behavior, whether in the school, neighborhood, workplace, or elsewhere.

The heart of this book has been an assessment of contemporary character education. Previous chapters have set out an argument that its theory and practice contain some serious flaws. Substantial changes to theory and practice were presented as a response to current inadequacies, primarily the lack of a developmental perspective. This reconstructed view is called developmental character education and I have argued that it overcomes the weaknesses of the current approach.

At its theoretical heart, developmental character education presents a more complete and sophisticated understanding of value issues and their connection to human understanding and behavior. At this core is the argument that the true moral life does not consist of simple or mindless obedience to some codified moral authority or rule book. Developmental character education incorporates the conviction that there is no "Encyclopedia of Morally Right Behavior for All Situations." It understands that it must be devoted to the aim of promoting persons capable of being, and inclined to be, autonomously thoughtful about moral value issues and how they should be decided and acted upon. Assumed as well is the critical role of moral principles in the making of sound judgments.

A FINAL COMMENT

The reader should not be surprised to find that I believe the theory and practice of developmental character education outlined in this book to be the most compelling approach to character education available. I am persuaded that this case is the soundest platform from which to generate curriculum and instruction in character education.

It also should be clear that this is not intended to be an instructional methods text. The examples of curriculum and instruction provided are samples of what I have derived from the theory and rationale presented. Curriculum designers, teachers, and others surely will derive and organize many more. There is no official instructional manual for developmental character education. The intelligence and local knowledge of school personnel must be employed to create the most effective developmental character education for their communities.

References

Althof, W., & Berkowitz, M. (2006, December). Moral education and character education: Their relationship and roles in citizenship education. *Journal of Moral Education, 35*(4), 495–518.

Bennett, W. J. (1993). *The index of leading cultural indicators.* Washington, DC: The
Heritage Foundation.

Bennett, W. J. (1996). *The book of virtues for young people: A treasury of great moral
stories.* Englewood Cliffs, NJ: Silver Burdett Press.

Benninga, J. S., & Wynne, E. W. (1998, February). Keeping in character: A time-tested
solution. *Phi Delta Kappan, 79*, 439–445.

Berkowitz, M. W., & Bier, M. C. (2005). *What works in character education: A report for
policy makers and the media.* Washington, DC: Character Education Partnership.

Berman, S. H. (1997). *Children's social consciousness and the development of social responsibility.* Albany: SUNY Press.

Berman, S. H. (2004, September). Teaching civics: A call to action. *Principal Leadership,
5*(1), 16–20.

Beyer, B. K. (1976, April). Conducting moral discussions in the classroom. *Social Education, 40*(4), 194–202.

Blatt, M., & Kohlberg, L. (1971). The effects of classroom discussion on the development of moral judgment. *Journal of Moral Education, 4*(2), 129–161.

Brooks, B. D., & Kann, M. E. (1963, November). What makes character education programs work. *Educational Leadership, 551*(3), 19–21.

Burgess, A. (1962). *A clockwork orange.* London: Heinemann.

Callahan, D. (2004). *The cheating culture: Why more Americans are doing wrong to get
ahead.* New York: Harcourt.

Catalano, R. F., Berglund, M. L., Ryan, J. A. M., Lonczak, H. S., & Hawkins, J. D. (2004,
January). Positive youth development in the United States: Research findings on
evaluations of positive youth development programs. *The ANNALS of the American Academy of Political and Social Science, 591*, 98–124.

Cross, B. (1997). What inner-city children say about character. In A. Molnar (Ed.), *The
construction of children's character* (pp. 120–126). Chicago: University of Chicago
Press.

Davis, M. (2003, November). What's wrong with character education. *American Journal of Education, 110*(1), 32–57.

Elam, S. M., Rose, L. C., & Gallup, A. M. (1993, October). The 25th annual Phi Delta
Kappa/Gallup poll of the public's attitudes toward the public schools. *Phi Delta
Kappan, 75*(2), 137–152.

Erikson, E. (1963). *Childhood and society.* New York: W. W. Norton.

Center for Civic Education. (December 2004). *From classroom to citizen: American attitudes on civic education.* Calabasas, CA: Author.

Gee, R., & Quick, J. (1997). *The Wisconsin citizenship initiative program guide*. Madison: Wisconsin Department of Public Instruction.

Gielen, U. (1991). Research on moral reasoning. In L. Kuhmerker (Ed.), *The Kohlberg legacy for the helping professions* (pp. 39–60). Birmingham, AL: R.E.P. Books.

Gilligan, C. (1982). *In a different voice*. Cambridge, MA: Harvard University Press.

Golding, W. (1954). *Lord of the flies*. New York: Perigee.

Hart, D., & Carlo, G. (2005). Moral development in adolescence. *Journal of Research on Adolescents, 15*(3), 223–233.

Hartshorne, H., & May, M. A. (1928). *Studies in deceit*. New York: Macmillan.

Heartwood Institute. (1992). *An ethics curriculum for children*. Pittsburgh, PA: The Heartwood Institute.

Henning, J. E. (2008). *The art of discussion-based teaching*. New York: Routledge.

Hoffman, M. L. (2000). *Empathy and moral development: Implications for caring and justice*. Cambridge, UK: Cambridge University Press.

Jackson, P. W. (1990). *Life In classrooms*. New York: Teachers College Press.

Josephson Institute of Ethics. (2006). *The ethics of American youth*. http://www.josephsoninstitute.org/

Kamtekar, R. (2004, April). Situationism and virtue ethics on the content of our character. *Ethics, 114*, 458–491.

Kohlberg, L. (1969). Stage and sequence: The cognitive-developmental approach to socialization. In D. Goslin (Ed.), *Handbook of socialization theory and research* (pp. 347–480). Chicago: Rand McNally.

Kohlberg, L. (1970). Education for justice: A modern statement of the Platonic view. In T. Sizer (Ed.), *Moral education: Five lectures* (pp. 57–83). Cambridge, MA: Harvard University Press.

Kohlberg, L. (1971). From is to ought: How to commit the naturalistic fallacy and get away with it in the study of moral development. In T. Mischel (Ed.), *Cognitive development and epistemology* (pp. 151–236). New York: Academic Press.

Kohlberg, L. (1973, October). The claim to moral adequacy of a highest stage of moral judgment. *Journal of Philosophy, 70*(18), 630–646.

Kohlberg, L. (1976). Moral stages and moralization: The cognitive–developmental approach. In T. Lickona (Ed.), *Moral development and behavior: Theory, research, and social issues* (pp. 31-53). New York: Holt, Rinehart and Winston.

Kohlberg, L. (1980). High school democracy and educating for a just society. In R. L. Mosher (Ed.), *Moral education: A first generation of research and development* (pp. 20–57). New York: Praeger.

Kohn, A. (1993). *Punished by rewards*. Boston, MA: Houghton-Mifflin.

Kohn, A. (1997, February). How not to teach values: A critical look at character education. *Phi Delta Kappan, 78*(6), 428–459.

LaPiere, R. T. (1970). Attitudes vs. actions. In D. Forcese & S. Richer (Eds.), *Stages of social research: Contemporary perspectives* (pp. 93–100). Englewood Cliffs, NJ: Prentice-Hall.

Leming, J. S. (1996). Teaching values in social studies education: Past practices and future possibilities. In B. Massialas & R. Allen (Eds.), *Crucial issues in the social studies* (pp. 145–180). Belmont, CA: Wadsworth.

Leming, J. S. (1997). Research and practice in character education: A historical perspective. In A. Molnar (Ed.), *The construction of children's character* (31–24). Chicago: University of Chicago Press.

Leming, J. S. (December, 2000). Tell me a story: An evaluation of a literature-based character education programme. *Journal of Moral Education, 29*(4), 413–427.

Leming, J. S. (2001, Spring/Summer). Historical and ideological perspectives on teaching moral and civic virtue. *The International Journal of Social Education, 16*(1), 62–76.

Lickona, T. (1976). Critical issues in the study of moral development and behavior. In T. Lickona (Ed.), *Moral development and behavior: Theory, research, and social issues* (pp. 3–27). New York: Holt, Rinehart and Winston.

Lickona, T. (1991). *Educating for character.* New York: Bantam Books.

Lickona, T. (1993, November). The return of character education. *Educational Leadership, 51*(3), 6–11.

Lickona, T. (1998, February). A more complex analysis is needed. *Phi Delta Kappan, 79*(6), 449–454.

Lickona, T. (2004). *Character matters: How to help our children develop good judgment, integrity, and other essential virtues.* New York: Simon & Schuster.

Lickona, T., & Davidson, M. (2005). *Smart and good high schools: Integrating excellence and ethics for success in school, work, and beyond.* Washington, DC: Character Education Partnership.

Lockwood, A. L. (1975, September). A critical view of values clarification. *Teachers College Record, 77*(1), 35–50.

Lockwood, A. L. (1985/1986). Keeping them in the courtyard: A response to Wynne. *Educational Leadership, 43*(4), 9–10.

Lockwood, A. L. (1993, November). A letter to character educators. *Educational Leadership, 51*(3), 72–75.

Lockwood, A. L. (1996, January). Controversial issues: The teacher's crucial role. *Social Education, 60*(1), 28–31.

Lockwood, A. L. (1997). What is character education? In A. Molnar (Ed.), *The construction of children's character* (pp. 174–185). Chicago: University of Chicago Press.

Lockwood, A. L., & Harris, D. E. (1985). *Reasoning with democratic values: Ethical problems in United States history.* New York: Teachers College Press.

Macaulay, J., & Berkowitz, L. (Eds.). (1970). *Altruism and helping behavior: Social psychological studies of some antecedents and consequences.* New York: Academic Press.

Milgram, S. (1965, February). Some conditions of obedience and disobedience to authority. *Human Relations, 18*(1), 57–76.

Murphy, M. M. (2002). *Character education in America's blue ribbon schools.* Lanham, MD: Scarecrow Press.

Myrdal, G. (1944). *An American dilemma.* New York: Harper & Row.

Noddings, N. (2002). *Educating moral people.* New York: Teachers College Press.

Parker, W. C. (2003). *Teaching democracy: Unity and diversity in public life.* New York: Teachers College Press.

Peters, R. S. (1967). *Ethics and education.* Oakland, NJ: Scott, Foresman.

Piaget, J. (1965). *The moral judgment of the child.* New York: Free Press.

Piaget, J. (1970). *Genetic epistemology.* New York: Columbia University Press.

Pinker, S. (2008, January 13). The moral instinct. *The New York Times Magazine*, pp. 32–58.

Prothro, J., & Grigg, C. (1960, May). Fundamental principles of democracy: Bases of agreement and disagreement. *Journal of Politics, 22*(2), 276–294.

Purpel, D. E. (1997). The politics of character education. In A. Molnar (Ed.), *The construction of children's character* (pp. 140–153). Chicago: University of Chicago Press.

Raths, L. E., Harmin, M., & Simon, S. B. (1966). *Values and teaching.* Columbus, OH: Charles E. Merrill.

Reimer, J., Paolitto, E. P., & Hersh, R. H. (1983). *Promoting moral growth: From Piaget to Kohlberg.* New York: Longman.

Rest, J. R. (1986). *Moral development: Advances in research and theory.* New York: Praeger.

Ryan, K. (1981). *Questions and answers on moral education.* Bloomington, IN: Phi Delta Kappa Educational Foundation.

Ryan, K. (1989). In defense of character education. In L. Nucci (Ed.), *Moral development and character education* (pp. 3–17). Berkeley, CA: McCutchan.

Ryan, K. (1993, November). Mining the values in the curriculum. *Educational Leadership, 51*(3), 16–18.

Ryan, K., & Bohlin, K. E. (1999). *Building character in schools: Practical ways to bring moral instruction to life.* San Francisco: Jossey-Bass.

Selman, R. L. (2003). *The promotion of social awareness: Powerful lessons from the partnership of developmental theory and classroom practice.* New York: Russell Sage Foundation.

Simon, K. G. (2001). *Moral questions in the classroom: How to get kids to think deeply about real life and their schoolwork.* New Haven, CT: Yale University Press.

Simon, S. B., Howe, L. W., & Kirschenbaum, H. (1972). *Values clarification: A handbook of practical strategies for teachers and students.* New York: Hart.

Smagorinsky, P., & Taxel, J. (2005). *The discourse of character education: Culture wars in the classroom.* Mahwah, NJ: Erlbaum.

Superka, D. P., Ahrens, C., & Hedstrom, J. E. (1976). *Values education sourcebook.* Boulder, CO: Social Science Education Consortium.

Westie, F. (1965, August). The American dilemma: An empirical test. *American Sociological Review, 30*(4), 527–538.

Wright, R. (1996). *Black boy.* New York: Harper & Row.

Wynne, E. A. (1985/1986). The great tradition in education: Transmitting moral values. *Educational Leadership, 43*(4), 4–9.

Wynne, E. A. (1989). Transmitting traditional values in contemporary schools. In L. P. Nucci (Ed.), *Moral development and character education* (pp. 19–36). Chicago: University of Chicago Press.

Wynne, E. A. (1997). For character education. In A. Molnar (Ed.), *The construction of children's character* (pp. 63–76). Chicago: University of Chicago Press.

Wynne, E. A., & Ryan, K. (1997). *Reclaiming our schools: Teaching character, academics, and discipline.* Columbus, OH: Merrill.

Wynne, E. A., & Walberg, H. J. (1985/1986). The complementary goals of character development and academic excellence. *Educational Leadership, 43*(4), 15–18.

Index

Academic subject matter, 88, 89
Althof, W., 78
Aristotle, 16, 30, 31
Autonomy vs. shame and denial stage, 49, 53, 54

Behavior
    and aim of character education, 2–3, 12
    autonomous, 71, 78
    and criticisms of character education, 13,
        14–15, 21, 22–25
    and definition of character education,
        69, 100
    and developmental curriculum content, 87
    and developmental instructional
        practices, 90, 92, 93
    and features of developmental character
        education, 71–73
    and goals of developmental character
        education, 70, 71, 78, 79
    and importance of developmental
        character education, 101
    and Kohlberg's developmentalism, 58
    and moral development, 11
    and need for character education, 3–4
    and responses to criticisms, 38, 39, 41
    societal influences on, 38
    and theory of developmental character
        education, 78, 79
    and values, 12, 16, 19–20, 21, 22–25, 33,
        38, 39, 41, 52, 69, 71–73, 78, 79, 82, 90,
        92, 93, 101
    and Values Clarification versus character
        education, 7
Behaviorism, 26–29, 33, 64
Bennett, William J., 3, 82
Benninga, Jacques, 2–3, 35, 37
Berglund, M. L., 15
Berkowitz, L., 23
Berkowitz, M., 78, 97
Berman, S. H., 88
Beyer, B. K., 75
Bier, M. C., 97
Blatt, Moshe, 11, 60
Bohlin, K. E., 97
Brooks, B. D., 26
Burgess, Anthony, 64

Callahan, D., 28
Carlo, G., 2
Catalano, R. F., 15
Change, criticisms as leading to, 36–37, 44,
    100, 101
Character education. *See also* Developmental
    character education; *specific person or topic*
    aim/goals of contemporary, 2–3, 12, 25, 46
    criticisms of, 3–5, 13–33, 71–77
    definition of, 1–12, 68–69, 77, 99–100
    leaders of, 2
    means of, 5–6
    moral development versus, 10–11
    need for, 2, 3–4
    "official" theory of learning in, 26–29
    responses to criticisms about, 34–44, 71–77
    Values Clarification versus, 6–11
    what is, 1–13, 99–100
Choice, personal, 6, 71–73
Citizenship, 64, 69–70, 78–79, 88, 100, 101
Classroom climate, 8
A Clockwork Orange (Burgess), 64
Cognitive developmentalism
    and developmental curriculum content,
        82, 85–86
    and developmental instructional practices,
        91–92
    of Kohlberg, 54–66
Context. *See also* Social context
    and criticisms of character education, 15, 33
    and developmental curriculum content,
        87–88, 89
    and developmentalism, 60
    and features of developmental character
        education, 71–73
    and human nature, 37, 38–39
    and need for character education, 3–4
    and responses to criticisms, 37, 38–39
    and Values Clarification versus character
        education, 7
Cooperative learning, 5, 6, 53–54
Creative writing, 94
Crime/criminals, 19–20, 43, 64, 76
Criticisms
    accuracy of, 35
    assessing soundness of, 35–37

Criticisms (*continued*)
    and change/modification in theory or
        rationale, 36–37, 44, 100, 101
    derivation of, 36
    and developmentalism, 31–32, 33
    of general theory, 13–21, 32–33, 37–44
    how to respond to, 34–35
    of psychological assumptions, 13, 15,
        22–31, 33
    responses to, 34–44
Cross, B., 25
Cross-age teaching/tutoring, 94, 97
Culture, and moral development, 62
Curriculum
    and conflicting values, 76
    and definition of character education, 69
    for developmental character education,
        80–89
    and developmentalism, 47
    and features of developmental character
        education, 73, 76
    and Kohlberg's contribution to character
        education, 66
    and meaning of values, 73
    and theory of developmental character
        education, 79

Davidson, M., 26, 88, 98
Davis, M., 30
Democracy, 4, 6, 101
Developmental character education
    aims/goals of, 70–71, 78, 79, 90
    curriculum content for, 80–89
    definition of, 68–70, 77
    in elementary school, 81–84, 92–93
    features of, 71–77
    highlights of theory of, 77–78
    instructional practices for, 89–97
    for middle and high school, 84–89, 91–92,
        93–94
    need for, 78–79
    overview of, 101
    theory of, 68–79
    value of, 100–101
Developmentalism
    and context, 60
    and criticisms of character education,
        31–32, 33
    and definition of character education, 69
    of Erikson, 48–54, 59–60, 67

    and formation of developmental
        perspective, 45–67
    and identity, 49–50, 51, 52, 53–54
    implications for character education of,
        51–54
    and instruction, 47, 60, 65, 66, 67
    Kohlberg's expansion of, 54, 56–66, 67
    and moral philosophy, 62–63
    and moral reasoning, 57–61, 62, 63, 64
    need for perspective of, 45–47, 66–67
    overview of, 47–48
    philosophical characteristics of, 62–63
    Piaget's influence on, 54–55, 56, 60
    psychological properties of stages of,
        59–62
    and responses to criticisms, 42, 43–44
Dilemmas. *See* Heinz dilemma; Moral
    dilemmas; Sharon's dilemma
Discussions
    conclusions to, 96–97
    and criticisms of character education, 26
    and developmental instructional practices,
        89, 93, 94–97
    in diverse settings, 101
    effective leading of, 95–97
    and features of developmental character
        education, 74, 75, 77
    "fish bowl", 96
    formats for, 96
    good, 95
    importance of, 26, 94–95
    and Kohlberg's contribution to character
        education, 64–65, 66
    major points made during, 95
    purpose of, 95
    and responses to criticisms, 41, 42
    on role of moral principles, 42
    teachers' role in, 96–97
Diversity, 101

Educational perspective. *See*
    Developmentalism
Ego integrity vs. despair stage, 50
Elementary schools, developmental character
    education in, 81–84, 90–91, 92–93
Empathy, 65–66
Environmental factors. *See* Context
Erikson, Erik, 48–54, 59–60, 67, 82
Ethical relativism, 8, 9–10, 12, 66
Ethics, 65, 70, 71, 72, 73, 78

"Fish bowl" discussions, 96
Freud, Anna, 48

Gee, R., 40
General theory. *See also* Human nature; Values
   criticisms of, 13–21, 32–33
   responding to criticisms of, 37–44
Generativity vs. stagnation stage, 50, 62
Gielen, U., 61
Gilligan, Carol, 47–48
The Godfather (novel and film), 19
Golding, William, 14
Good character, 3–4, 5–6, 12, 13
Goodness, and Kohlberg's developmentalism, 58
"Great tradition", 4, 16, 40
Grigg, C., 24

Habituation, 29, 30–31, 33
Harmin, M., 6, 7, 8
Harris, D. E., 19, 86
Hart, D., 2
Hartshoren, Hugh, 22, 24
Hawkins, J. D., 15
Heartwood Institute, 81
Heinz dilemma, 10, 18, 56–57, 58, 59, 85
Henning, J. E., 96
Hersh, R. H., 18
High school, developmental character
   education for, 84–89, 91–92, 93–94
Hobbes, Thomas, 14
Hoffman, M. L., 66
Howe, L. W., 8, 9
Human nature, 14–15, 33, 37–39

Identity, 49–50, 51, 52, 53–54
Identity vs. role confusion stage, 49–50, 52, 54
Indoctrination, 14, 66, 79
Industry vs. inferiority stage, 49, 53, 54
Initiative vs. guilt stage, 49, 54
Institutional constraints, 88
Instruction. *See also* Teaching
   civic, 69–70
   and conflicting values, 76
   and criticisms of character education, 13–14
   and definition of character education, 69
   for developmental character education, 89–97
   and developmentalism, 47, 60, 65, 66, 67
   didactic, 89

and features of developmental character
   education, 73, 76
and human nature, 14
and Kohlberg's contribution to character
   education, 65, 66
and meaning of values, 73
for promoting good character, 5–6, 12
and theory of developmental character
   education, 79
and Values Clarification versus character
   education, 8, 9
Instrumental-relativist orientation stage, 58
Integrity vs. despair stage, 62
Internet, 94
Intimacy vs. isolation stage, 50

Josephson Institute of Ethics, 24
Journal of Research in Character Education, 1
Journals, 92, 93, 97

Kamtekar, R., 41
Kann, M. E., 26
Kant, Immanuel, 16, 20, 40
Kirschenbaum, H., 8, 9
Kohlberg, Lawrence, 10–11, 18, 24, 48, 54–66, 67
Kohn, A., 14, 27, 28

LaPiere, Richard T., 23–24
Law and order stage, 58
Leming, J. S., 22, 60, 73, 81
Lickona, Thomas, 2, 3–4, 5–6, 9–10, 13, 22, 26, 32, 35, 42, 88, 97, 98
Literature, 82–83, 86
Lockwood, A. L., 6, 9, 12, 15–16, 18, 19, 25, 30, 31, 86, 96
Lonczak, H. S., 15

Macaulay, J., 23
May, Mark, 22, 24
Methods. *See* Instruction
Middle school, developmental character
   education for, 84–89, 91–92, 93–94
Milgram, S., 23
Mill, John Stuart, 16, 40
Mock trials, 94
Modeling, 5–6, 29–30, 33
Moral action, 4, 61, 70
Moral authority, 77, 78, 101
Moral development. *See also* Kohlberg,
   Lawrence; Piaget, Jean

Moral development (*continued*)
   character education versus, 10–11
   and culture, 62
   and Erikson's developmentalism, 51, 52–53, 54
   and ethical relativism, 66
   and goals of developmental character education, 70, 71
Moral development (*continued*)
   importance of, 71
   of Kohlberg, 56–66
   and perspective taking, 61
   of Piaget, 55
   psychology of, 10–11
   stages of, 10–11, 56–59
   and Values Clarification, 10–11
Moral dilemmas, 10, 11, 18–19, 56–57, 61, 65, 76–77, 86, 91, 95. *See also* Heinz dilemma; Sharon's dilemma; Values: conflicting
Moral education, paradox of, 31
Moral feeling, as component of good character, 4
Moral judgments, 61, 62, 63, 83, 86–87, 88–89, 91, 101
Moral knowing, as component of good character, 4
Moral principles
   and criticisms of character education, 33
   and developmental curriculum content, 86, 88
   and features of developmental character education, 76–77
   identification and discussion of, 42, 86
   and importance of developmental character education, 101
   and responses to criticisms, 39, 42–43
   role in character education of, 21, 39, 42–43, 76–77, 86, 88
Moral reasoning, 11, 57–61, 62, 63, 64
Moral values, 3, 4, 8–9, 11, 15–21, 74, 76, 84–85, 88
Murphy, M. M., 26
Myrdal, Gunnar, 18

Naturalistic fallacy, 62
Noddings, Nel, 48
Nonmoral values, 8–9, 84–85, 88
Nonschool settings, character education in, 97, 100

Paolitto, E. P., 18
Parker, W. C., 96
Perspective-taking, 61, 65, 66, 70, 83, 86–87, 88–89, 90–91, 92, 93
Peters, R. S., 31
Philosophical aspects, 14–15, 33, 37–39, 62–63, 74, 78, 84–85
Piaget, Jean, 10, 48, 54–55, 56, 60, 63
Pinker, Steven, 84
Plato, 16
Privacy rights, of students, 92–93
Prothro, J., 24
Psychological factors, 10–11, 13, 15, 22–31, 33, 56–66, 73, 78. *See also* Developmentalism
Punishment, 26–29, 82
Punishment and obedience stage, 57
Purpel, D. E., 3, 15

Quick, J., 40

Raths, L. E., 6, 7, 8
Reason/reasoning, 31, 57–59, 60–61, 62, 63, 82. *See also* Moral reasoning
Reimer, J., 18
Religion, 7, 63
Respect, 4, 8, 16, 29–30, 55, 73, 74, 76, 83, 85
Responsibility, 4, 15, 16, 33, 37, 38–39, 48, 72, 73
Rest, J. R., 72
Rewards, 26–29
Role playing, 89–92
Ryan, J. A. M., 15
Ryan, Kevin, 2, 3, 5, 11, 22, 26, 27, 29, 30–31, 32, 88, 97

Schools, importance of promotion of character education by, 100–101
Self-enteredness, 3, 5, 28, 64
Self-concept, 50
Self-esteem, 5
Self-interest, 57, 63, 64, 77, 82
Selman, Robert, 61, 64
Sharon's dilemma, 75–77, 87, 91
Should-would concepts, 72–73, 87, 95
Simon, K. G., 43, 88, 96
Simon, S. B., 6, 7, 8, 9
Simon, Theodore, 55

Social context
  and criticisms of character education,
    14–15, 20, 33
  and features of developmental character
    education, 71–73, 76
  and human nature, 37, 38–39
  and need for character education, 3–4
  and responses to criticisms, 37, 38–39
  and role of moral principles in character
    education, 76
  and theory of developmental character
    education, 78
  and understanding of values, 78
  and Values Clarification versus character
    education, 7
Social contract orientation, 58
"The Sopranos" (TV), 19
Statistics, 3
Strategies, 8, 9

Teachers
  and criticisms of character education,
    29–30, 33
  and developmental curriculum content, 88
  institutional constraints on, 88
  and Kohlberg's contribution to character
    education, 64, 66
  modeling by, 29–30, 33
  role in developmental curriculum content
    of, 85
  role in discussions of, 96–97
  as role models, 5–6
  role in teaching moral values of, 11
  students' perceptions of, 30
  and Values Clarification versus character
    education, 8
Teaching. *See also* Instruction
  and criticisms of character education,
    22, 25–29
  cross-age, 94, 97
Trust vs. mistrust stage, 49, 53, 82

Universal ethical principle orientation, 58

Value judgments, 90, 93
Values. *See also specific topic*
  application to life circumstances of, 19
  assessment of, 70–71, 81
  and behavior, 12, 16, 19–20, 21, 22–25,
    33, 38, 39, 41, 52, 69, 71–73, 78, 79, 82,
    90, 92, 93, 101
  conflicting, 18–19, 21, 31, 33, 39, 41, 42,
    75–77, 86, 88
  consensus about, 13, 20–21, 33, 39–40,
    74
  and criticisms of character education, 13,
    15–21, 22–25
  and definition of character education,
    69, 100
  definition/meaning of, 7–8, 16–18, 21, 39,
    41, 43, 73–75, 76, 78, 79, 81, 83, 92
  and developmental curriculum content,
    81–89
  and developmental instructional
    practices, 93
  and developmentalism, 42
  and features of developmental character
    education, 71–76
  and goals of developmental character
    education, 70–71
  and identification of value issues, 81–82,
    83–84, 85, 88, 90
  lists of, 16–17, 40, 43, 73–75
  and need for character education, 4
  neutrality of, 8–9
  prior, 25, 33
  and response to criticisms, 39–43, 44
  role of moral principles in developing,
    21, 39, 42–43, 76–77, 86, 88
  as supportive of objectionable or
    questionable behavior, 19–20
  teaching of, 22, 25–29
  and theory of developmental character
    education, 78, 79
  vocabulary of, 81
  worthwhile, 82, 84
Values Clarification
  character education versus, 6–11
  and Moral Development, 10–11

Walberg, H. J., 22, 29, 88
Westie, F., 24
Wright, Richard, 91
Writing assignments, 92–94
Wynne, Edward, 2, 3, 4, 5, 11, 14, 16, 22, 26,
  27, 29, 30, 35, 37, 39–40, 88

About the Author

Alan L. Lockwood received his undergraduate degree from Syracuse University and his master's and doctoral degrees from the Harvard Graduate School of Education. He is currently a Professor of Curriculum and Instruction at the University of Wisconsin–Madison.

Professor Lockwood has written extensively on the topics of Values Clarification, moral education, and character education. In addition to his interests in these topics, he is also the coordinator of secondary teacher education at the University of Wisconsin–Madison and is directly involved with social studies education.

This volume is based on his many years of research on the general topic of values education and reflects his critical views of the various approaches that have been brought forward. It is his hope that *The Case for Character Education* will provide guidance for improving the theory and practice of character education programs in the schools.